ACCESS TO SUCCESS AND SOCIAL MOBILITY THROUGH HIGHER EDUCATION

Great Debates in Higher Education is a series of short, accessible books addressing key challenges to and issues in higher education (HE), at a national and international level. These books are research informed but debate driven. They are intended to be relevant to a broad spectrum of researchers, students and administrators in HE, and are designed to help us unpick and assess the state of higher education systems, policies, and social and economic impacts.

ACCESS TO SUCCESS AND SOCIAL MOBILITY THROUGH HIGHER EDUCATION

A CURATE'S EGG?

EDITED BY

STUART BILLINGHAM
York St John University, UK

United Kingdom – North America – Japan – India
Malaysia – China

Emerald Publishing Limited
Howard House, Wagon Lane, Bingley BD16 1WA, UK

First edition 2018

Reprints and permissions service
Contact: permissions@emeraldinsight.com

British Library Cataloguing in Publication Data
A catalogue record for this book is available from the British
Library

ISBN: 978-1-78754-110-8 (paperback)
ISBN: 978-1-78743-836-1 (E-ISBN)
ISBN: 978-1-78743-992-4 (Epub)

ISOQAR certified
Management System,
awarded to Emerald
for adherence to
Environmental
standard
ISO 14001:2004.

Certificate Number 1985
ISO 14001

INVESTOR IN PEOPLE

CONTENTS

SECTION C
INNOVATIONS IN ACCESS
TO SUCCESS

SECTION D
ACCESS TO SUCCESS AND
SOCIAL MOBILITY: THINKING BIG

FOREWORD

The story of widening participation and promoting social mobility to and through higher education (HE), so powerfully illustrated in this volume, has a proud history, where leaders and players have come together at different times and in different places to forge new ways of engaging social change. In charting our successes, partial successes and unfinished business, it is salutary to look back on half a century of what we popularly term 'struggle' but is in practice a now normalised way of aligning people, places and political action through creative educational strategies that aspire to promote progress for the many not the few.

My personal story begins in 1973 as a 'mature'[1] student and parent at the University of Surrey – this, the re-housed and re-badged Battersea Polytechnic Institute, which began life in 1891, offering science and technology to the 'poorer inhabitants' of London. Six years later, I moved to my first, short-term contract-researcher post in the Polytechnics world – at the famous Polytechnic of North London (PNL). This drew on the combined and powerful legacies of the Northern Polytechnic Institute (1896), 'promoting the technical skill, general knowledge, health and wellbeing of young men and

---

1 The now-familiar descriptor 'mature' was neither articulated, nor conceptually understood in the early 1970s.

women'; and the North Western Polytechnic focussing on social sciences, humanities and arts.

In the 1990s, I progressed to Sheffield Hallam University (SHU) with its traditions firmly rooted in regional development. The Sheffield School of Design was founded in 1843 'to provide skilled designers to support Britain's industries'. Finally, in 1999, I joined the College of Ripon and York St John as Principal. The College would become York St John University, but would never neglect its nineteenth century mission, shaped by the Dioceses of York and of Ripon, to construct a cadre of teachers imbued with moral rectitude and high levels of learning, who would educate and create opportunity for the children of the poor.

Importantly, these staging posts in my career suggest that the twenty-first century universities are, literally, well placed to build on firm foundations, translating Victorian educational legacies into a contemporary vision for an inclusive society. The appetite for this challenge, however, clearly varies across institutions. Arguably, it is through leadership at all levels that we realise the vision of HE's founding fathers.

The 1980s will not be recalled as a period in which public services were best placed to secure the public benefit demanded by their communities. The phrase 'rolling back of the welfare state' became a *leit motif* for savage financial cuts to local services; marketisation; strangely, centralisation of control; and a lurch towards a form of harsh modernisation experienced by many as a negation of past contributions to community wellbeing. The PNL was not isolated from such a change.

Notwithstanding the dismantling of the Greater London Council (GLC), we did initially retain the unquestioning support of the Inner London Education Authority (ILEA). A particular lead by ILEA, then the HE funder for inner London Polytechnics, was sponsoring access through a generous budgetary allocation to the five HEIs for 'affirmative action funding'.[2] This annual budget line was not hypothecated for particular activities – but it was, of course, accountable. At the PNL, this enabled working with our neighbouring Boroughs, particularly Islington, Haringey and Hackney, to address the aspirations of newer and diverse communities – African Caribbean, South Asian and Irish.

Accordingly, partnership and cross-agency working became the new norm and early innovation produced the first important tranche of social workers and teachers who reflected the experiences and ambitions of their own communities – supported by introductory Access programmes. As the fate of ILEA echoed that of the GLC, Polytechnics typically resolved (both within management and through the trade unions) to protect the ever-widening concept and practices of access and Access.

At the PNL, I was supported within Natfhe (the National Association of Teachers in Further and Higher Education, now UCU) to take on roles both within the Union and on the Board of Governors – which provided developmental opportunities both for me and for the PNL. As the Polytechnics Secretary for Natfhe's Inner London Regional Assembly, I was able to share and shape policy developments for part-time study in HE; for the establishment of research programmes in Polytechnics to underpin an excellent student experience (then a radical idea); and for the protection of budgets to acknowledge the needs and contribution of new kinds of learners (see also, e.g., Marr & Butcher in this volume, Chapter 4).

---

2 Following 1970s, equalities legislation, a tangible expression of political desire (by some) for a fairer society was the introduction of affirmative action strategies to support marginalised groups – as opposed to positive discrimination.

Looking at specific activity, it is not insignificant that the acclaimed access/Access work of the redoubtable Maggie Woodrow was located, at this time, at the PNL. Both a sponsor of well founded initiatives and a myth buster for inappropriate attempts to short-circuit necessary investments in social inclusivity, Maggie's early evaluation of two-year accelerated degrees aimed at mature and/or non-traditional students identified the significant barriers, both for students and HEIs, in achieving successful outcomes. As learning about widening participation started to accumulate, one important legacy from that optimistic moment when change seemed possible is the Irish Studies Centre at London Metropolitan University.[3]

In 2016, this small but influential exemplar of public benefit celebrated with the Irish Ambassador and the Leader of the Labour Party (among other eminent guests) a proud 30-year history, which has attracted global recognition. In 1986, as the PNL Director of Research, I secured support to establish the first University-level Centre to acknowledge and explore further, through teaching, research and community partnerships, the specific experiences (contributions and conflicts) of the Irish in Britain. This was not just through glorious literature, drama and history but as a force for productive economic and social change in the widest sense. This serves as a powerful signal of how scholarly excellence, university relevance and community benefit can come together when underpinned by the values and commitment of an institution to its continuing access mission (see also, e.g., Gaskell & Dunn, Chapter 12; Newton & Rowe, Chapter 10; Thomas in this volume, Chapter 14).

---

3 In 2002, the former PNL, subsequently University of North London, merged with London Guildhall University to become London Metropolitan University.

One of the lessons learned concerning effective leadership is to network, become visible and secure a positioning where you are noticed! This is not an endorsement of individual, aggressive self-promotion, but more a recognition that active pursuit of significant goals requires significant action.

Therefore, the access leadership journey does typically involve joining up different roles and relationships and placing access explicitly at the heart of them. When my junior research role at the PNL shifted to whole institution Director of Research in 1986, it enabled cross-faculty conversations and developments, always asserting excellence with relevance, and learning how that might be interpreted across disciplines and delivered with an access orientation. This, in turn, led to an invitation to join the Postgraduate Awards Panel of the Economic and Social Research Council. In addition, my concern with teaching excellence (and a new role as Faculty Dean) led to a position on the Council for National Academic Awards and a role as quality auditor with the Higher Education Quality Council – all places in which to confront access dilemmas. The mid-1990s, however, brought a new, political, clarion-call to pursue 'education, education, education....'[4]

Helpfully, this post-dated the Polytechnics' shift of title to be named universities and secure greater autonomy. This enabled a new and positive dialogue for policy makers and practitioners alongside their partners in the communities they served. Arriving at SHU as Assistant Principal in 1993, I encountered a city and sub-region in transition. The language of 'industrial upheaval' fails to capture the deep decimation of traditional skill-based employment and community lifestyle around coal and steel. The urgent need to re-skill redundant workers and their children, and to meet the expectations of

---

4 The pre-election promise of New Labour.

the women who had developed new confidence and ambition as they supported their families through painful challenge and change, was high on the 'to-do' list of my new colleagues and collaborators in diverse outreach activities.

Access can appear in many guises. The Sheffield Hallam that I joined was both an instigator and an early adopter of much innovation. A particular leadership style espoused by the Vice Chancellor, John Stoddart, was 'to enable great people to do great things'. In other words, he facilitated through his senior team, his Board and his external connectivity, a permissive environment where participation in HE by the wider community was of primacy. The curriculum was designed in ways that would facilitate entry to the emerging economy of new technologies and cultural industries, yet also respected traditional strengths and excellence as in materials science and urban studies; it also supported public services. Entry to and success within the University was encouraged and enabled through:

- outreach in schools and further education;

- curriculum structure offering flexible study (an early example of combined studies that really worked for learners);

- the visibility and popularity of town and gown lectures; and

- the creation of a student-friendly, one-stop-shop support infrastructure building confidence and achievement across the student 'life-cycle': from 'getting in'; to 'getting through'; towards 'getting out' and getting a good graduate job; and ultimately getting 'back in' for further study.

The 1990s were especially important for highlighting gender difference in HE and exploring diverse ways to challenge

barriers, and improve opportunities for women. SHU was one
of the first Polytechnics/Universities to introduce and achieve
scholarly recognition for Women's Studies – both within the
curriculum and as an area of research. In the City of Sheffield,
a motivational initiative called 'If I can, you can', brought
together women leaders for mutual support and, importantly,
to go into schools and support teachers and pupils.[5] Talks
with classes of girls (and often boys) generated unexpected
dialogue around what counts as being a leader and how do
I get there! Moreover, of course, it was in the 1990s that –
Through the Glass Ceiling – led by the exceptional Chris King
addressed the question 'Why are there so few women leaders in our universities'. Hence, the 'clarion call' from political
leaders found traction with SHU leaders and beyond. And
whilst a 50% participation rate in HE continues to underpin
the thought leadership of many government agencies today,
the new millennium would bring new challenges requiring
new vigilance and new resolution.

At this propitious moment, in mid-1999, I joined the College of Ripon and York St John as Principal. Tellingly, a fellow (*sic*) Principal observed, warmly, whilst congratulating
me: 'Isn't it great to be running your own train set?' Therefore, this was the pivotal moment when I might draw upon
the influences and experiences of peers and mentors, projects
and partnerships across my former university lives – and yet
remember that male imagery and metaphor had not yielded
up their grip with respect to ideas of leading change.

The decade began for me as a tale of two proud Cathedral
cities and two modest and unassuming Colleges of fading Victorian grandeur, Colleges that must merge into one in order to

---

5 Visits usually occurred as part of what was then tortuously badged,
   'PSHE' – Personal, Social and Health Education, now more commonly
   timetabled 'citizenship education'.

protect the values and mission of access for the wider community. In particular, there was a longstanding commitment that
was acknowledged tacitly, and would be nurtured further,
to open our doors (literally and metaphorically) to those for
whom HE had no self-evident attraction or relevance. Moreover, rationalisation to a single site in York would facilitate
change and growth. York with its world-class heritage, great
connectivity, glorious countryside and an exceptional tour-
ist draw was chosen as the future base for investment. Yet,
this beautiful city also concealed significant pockets of deprivation; and across the hinterland, an emerging imperative
towards rural and coastal access was highlighted by voices
from the soon-to-become York St John College, subsequently,
University (see also, e.g. Gaskell & Dunn, Chapter 12; Noble
& Grant in this volume, Chapter 5).

As a small college with a big agenda, partnership (both
of necessity and by choice) was at the heart of the forward
strategy – led by a senior team seriously skilled and experienced in the policy and practice of enabling social inclusion,
including the Editor of this text! The City of York, in dialogue,
supported plans for a fit-for-purpose campus regeneration to
support new learning styles and engage new learners. National HE agencies such as the Leadership Foundation (LFHE)
and the Higher Education Academy embraced and utilised
our expertise, both on their Boards but also as their train-
ers and facilitators – and as early entrants into the esteemed
hall of National Teaching Fellows. During the passage of the
Higher Education Act 2004, it was helpful to have the College Principal positioned as Chair of what is now GuildHE[6]
– working with Ministers to defend the best outcomes for the

---

6 The Standing Conference of Principals, founded in the 1970s, was one of
   two formal representative bodies for HE in the UK alongside what is now
   UUK. In 2006, it changed its name to GuildHE.

widest range of future students as the new and controversial tuition fees regime came into play. Importantly, this was mitigated, in part, by the introduction of a new regulatory force in the form of the Office for Fair Access.

Other partnerships at subject level, at professional level and around research interests ensured that the engagement of scholars from across the college contributed to the wider HE debates. For example, about what counts as widening opportunities for a particular subject, for the neighbourhood or city, and for the college/university. Importantly, this was not the task of a single heroic leader but one that was shared. One unifying theme which elicited different views and provoked different responses was our identity as a Church Foundation and its relevance for the social inclusivity agenda. A group of some 12 Church Colleges would meet under the banner of what came to be known as the Cathedrals Group in HE. For College leaders, this served as both a challenge and support group, exploring diverse policy and practice issues – including the boundaries of Church connectivity and the impact this might have on access missions, as subscribed to by all. In different geographies and different social contexts, it became clear that Christian values had underpinned significant thought leadership around access.

At York St John, the identification of faith advisers from seven world religions (seven women and seven men) contributed creatively to the understanding and celebration of diverse cultures for both a significantly white student community and a significantly white city. And it enabled successful outreach initiatives via workshops in West Yorkshire where Muslim mothers looked with confidence to York St John as a safe and respectful environment for their daughters. Yet, perhaps the most influential collaboration, shaped and sustained in large part by York St John, has been Higher York. This was the UK's second lifelong learning partnership and is still active today. Yet, it began very nervously with a secret meeting in a basement bar in York between three CEOs: from University of York, York FE College and York St John.

There was anxiety about status and excellence, takeover/ merger, standards dilution, mission distraction and loss of face – unspoken sentiments that might be attributed to academic communities rather than to the leaders themselves. In reality, the leaders had an emerging high ambition for a seamless education system available for York and North Yorkshire to offer students a comprehensive curriculum from (e.g.) Archaeology to Zoology – with scenic routes linking options and levels across institutions, as students journey towards their academic goals.

One measure of success is the swift move from project-plotting to consultation and effective bidding; then through to 'delivery' – with an enhanced membership to include the local agricultural college. A measure of impact is the naming and full incorporation of the work of Higher York into the City of York Local Strategic Plan where the virtues of widening access to HE for economic, social and cultural gain are explicitly articulated. And a measure of the positioning of York St John in this mix is the routine reference by civic leaders to 'our two universities' – where the particular access role of York St John is seen to complement the global reputation for research excellence of the University of York.

Meanwhile, in 2008, an exciting opportunity to forge new pathways and new thinking beyond York was secured through the Vice-Chancellor's membership of the HEFCE board and associated chairing of its Widening Access and Participation Committee. Notwithstanding the seemingly benign climate for HE engendered by the commitment to 'education, education, education', the economic clouds of financial failure were hovering over part-publically funded bodies as the decade was drawing to a close. Leading social inclusivity through uncertainty and turbulence became the watchword for success. Performance indicators for the opening of doors were threatened and, as my retirement beckoned, supporting the ambitions of the next generation of leaders became my key goal. As my Leadership Consultancy business cards arrived and the home office took shape, my retiree diary for 2010 started to reflect my continuing passion for challenge and change towards widening participation and social mobility. A social justice imperative links with my Trustee roles at the Joseph Rowntree Foundation, in Health and in the Arts. I have enjoyed developing for the LFHE their well-regarded Governor Development Programme. Moreover, I returned as an enthusiastic Trustee to the regenerating London Metropolitan University. Clearly, in diverse geographies and sectors, there exist multiple opportunities for shaping change.

This narrative demonstrates that leadership across different time frames can manifest itself in different places and in different ways – and that leadership qualities do not depend on status or title. In the case of widening participation, this is evidenced across this series of essays. We see that political and historical contexts help to shape the particular form that leading change will follow: whether operating under the radar of reactionary forces, or riding with the tide of good intentions! But an effective leader, in their turn, will seek to reinvent and shape that environment, for the better. Influence on social inclusivity is best exerted through positioning and partnerships where common interests unite governments, local or national, and where shared goals with arms-length-agencies, labour movement leaders, students, employers, fellow providers of FHE and many more can exert a multiplier effect on successful outcomes.

In conclusion, I observe that the 'Curate's Egg' of the title might be said to mask a sustained and often heroic series of endeavours that make a reality of access to success and social mobility through engagement with a rich and diverse community of protagonists. Inevitably, impact remains patchy (as signalled by the 'Curate's Egg' metaphor) and in part unproven but, most encouragingly, the appetite to address unfinished business is illustrated powerfully throughout this volume.

Professor Dianne Willcocks, CBE, DL

ABOUT THE CONTRIBUTORS

Dr Graeme Atherton Founder and Director of 'AccessHE' and the National Education Opportunities Network (NEON), has worked in the access to post-secondary education field for 20 years both in the UK and internationally. He is Visiting Professor at London Metropolitan University, Amity Business School and Sunway University Malaysia.

Professor Stuart Billingham is Professor Emeritus of Lifelong Learning at York St John University being previously Pro Vice Chancellor at the University. He has worked to widen access to success in, and through, tertiary education for almost 40 years. He has published widely, both nationally and internationally, and regularly presents at major international conferences on these issues.

Dr John Butcher is Associate Director (Curriculum & Access), Learning and Teaching Innovation, at The Open University. John has led research projects for the Office for Fair Access on outreach for disadvantaged adult learners, and for the Higher Education Academy (HEA) on part-time learning in higher education (HE). He is currently Co-Editor of the international journal *Widening Participation and Lifelong Learning* and is an executive member of the Forum for Access and Continuing Education (FACE).

Siobhan Clay is Educational Developer in the Teaching and Learning Exchange at University of the Arts London (UAL).

Her role is focused on student experience and attainment agendas, working with academics to support inclusive pedagogies and curriculum development. Siobhan has taught on the *Inclusivity* unit of the Postgraduate Certificate in Teaching and Learning (PG Cert) for staff, and has supervised colleagues undertaking diversity and inclusion research projects.

Louis Coiffait is Associate Editor at Wonkhe, where he: writes, commissions and edits articles; produces email briefings and speaks at a range of events. He also leads on a number of new partnerships, consultancy and services. He has researched a wide range of education policy topics, including; access to HE, apprenticeships, employability, careers and selection. His career includes working with Reform, NFER, Pearson, TTA, HEA, for an MP and a Government Minister.

Ian Dunn is Deputy Vice Chancellor (Student Experience) at Coventry University. Ian's success in the 2016 *Guardian* Higher Education Awards 'Inspiring Leader' category sums up the way he works with colleagues, students and the local community alike, and he is a driving force behind a number of prestigious additions to the University's widening participation portfolio – most recently CU Scarborough and CU Coventry.

Professor Craig Gaskell is Professor of Higher Education Enterprise and Associate Pro Vice Chancellor at Coventry University. He was founding Provost of CU Scarborough, Coventry's new start-up campus on the Yorkshire coast, leading the project from initial concept to full implementation. He has extensive experience of senior management and leading change in the university sector. His research interests include organisational forms and student experience in Higher Education, enabling close alignment between his research and professional practice.

Professor Dwight E. Giles, Jr is Professor Emeritus of Higher Education at the University of Massachusetts, Boston, USA. Dwight was recently inducted into the Academy of Community Engagement Scholarship. He has been a practitioner-scholar of Experiential Education for 35 years, during which time he has taught courses and directed programmes in service-learning and international internships. He has co-authored numerous books and articles on service-learning research and community engagement including '*Where's the Learning in Service-Learning?*'.

Jessica Grant has been based at the University of Tasmania since March 2014 working across strategic planning and government engagement functions. Previously, she was Director of the Higher York Lifelong Learning Network in the UK, working on a range of widening participation projects, including Aimhigher. Prior to this, Jessica worked with post-16 providers to develop lifelong learning provision across York and North Yorkshire, for the Learning and Skills Council.

Clara Gwatirera is an education activist whose work in South Africa focusses on youth empowerment and development, and the promotion of educational opportunities for orphaned and vulnerable children. In 2005, she was a young person representative for Zimbabwe to the UN Secretary General's study on violence against children. In 2011, she was a delegate at the One Young World Summit in Switzerland. Clara aspires to study theology in the near future, and currently works as a Sales Consultant in Johannesburg.

Dr Mark Jones is Chief Operating Officer at Advance HE, formerly the Higher Education Academy (HEA). Prior to joining the HEA in 2014, Mark worked on the development of digital learning and digital curriculum materials, in the development of web-based delivery of public services (including launching the NHS's first app), and in a range of business development roles across the private and charity sectors.

Dr Liz Marr is Director of Teaching at the Open University, UK, having originally joined the University as Director of the Centre for Widening Participation. She has a long history of engagement with the widening participation agenda in the UK, initially through the Aimhigher programme. She is Co-Editor of the international *Journal of Widening Participation and Lifelong Learning* and Chair of the Action on Access Forum.

Dr Helen May works at Advance HE (formerly the Higher Education Academy), currently leading Teaching Excellence Awards. Over the last 13 years, she has led a number of priority themes, including social capital, internationalisation, change, inclusion, retention and widening participation. An experienced teacher and educational researcher, Helen authored a National framework for enhancing student success (2016) and published in 2017 on communities of practice.

Nik Miller is Chief Executive of the Bridge Group and Director at More Partnership. Prior to this, he worked in the USA, at the University of Warwick and the University of York. Nik has advised the UK Government on social mobility, and collaborated with a range of organisations to support more equal access to HE and the professions, including Google, KPMG, the University of Oxford, the Wellcome Trust, the BBC and Trinity College Dublin.

Dr Neil Murray is Associate Professor of Applied Linguistics at the University of Warwick, UK, and an adjunct member of the Research Centre for Languages and Cultures at the University of South Australia (UniSA). Previously, he co-convened the 1st International Australasian Conference on Enabling Access to Higher Education, which led to the publication of *Aspiration Access and Attainment: International* *perspectives on widening participation: an agenda for change* (Routledge 2014, with Chris Klinger).

Simon Newton is a Charity Trustee and activist. He is currently Trustee of *Out of Character*, a theatre company whose members have used mental health services, and *Pilot Theatre*, an international touring company aimed at young adults. He was Deputy Director of Communications at the Open University, Director of Enterprise and Innovation at the University of York and Head of Partnerships at York St John University.

Professor Margaret Noble is Pro Vice-Chancellor (Academic Quality and Schools Engagement) at the University of Tasmania. Previously, she was Chief Executive at Waiariki Institute of Technology in New Zealand and at the now University of St Mark and St John in the UK. She has directed a number of large regional widening participation projects in the North East of England and South East London, and led the establishment of the Kent and Medway Lifelong Learning Network. Margaret has published widely in urban and regional studies, higher education policy and widening participation.

Dr Nick Rowe is Associate Professor at York St John University and Director of 'Converge' – an initiative offering higher educational opportunities to people who use mental health services, which he founded in 2008 and now being adopted by the Universities in Leeds and Newcastle. Nick trained as a psychiatric nurse and dramatherapist. Since the launch of Converge he has written extensively about the model and the lessons to be learned from it.

Dr Bruria Schaedel is Senior Lecturer at the Western Galilee Project, Akko, Israel. She is Founder, Director and Senior Researcher of several projects at the University of Haifa and the Western Galilee College. 'The Western Gallts' project aimed to develop cooperation and partnerships among Jews and Arabs in the northern region. The mutual partnerships were developed in various groups and included children, teachers, parents and students.

Dr Gerard Sharpling is Senior Teaching Fellow within the Centre for Applied Linguistics, University of Warwick. He has previously worked for the Open University, the University of Birmingham and the Faculté des Lettres et Sciences Humaines, Université de Nantes (France). His main current areas of interest lie in English for Academic Purposes and Language Testing. He is particularly interested in empowering students from diverse linguistic and social backgrounds by helping them to develop their writing.

Dr Tim Stanton is Senior Associate/Engaged Scholar for Ravensong Associates (USA), through which he consults in global service-learning design, development and research in the United States, Africa and Asia. In 2016, Tim was Visiting Professor in International Studies at Northwestern University (USA). He is a Director Emeritus of Stanford University's Bing Overseas Studies Program in Cape Town, South Africa. He has published numerous articles and two books on service learning and engaged scholarship.

Emilie Sundorph was a Researcher at the think tank *Reform,* at the time of contributing to the writing of the first chapter in this volume. At *Reform,* she worked on a wide range of themes, including how top universities can be held accountable for supporting social mobility. Prior to working at *Reform,* Emilie worked with a number of educational charities, including Prisoners' Education Trust and The Challenge. She is now at Teach First.

Professor Liz Thomas is Professor of Higher Education at Edge Hill University and an independent consultant. She has approximately 20 years' experience of undertaking and managing research about widening participation, student retention and success and institutional approaches to improving the student experience and outcomes. She is author and editor of over 10 books, many journal articles, reports, briefings and practice guides – all informing institutional, national and international policy and practice.

Danail Vasilev was a Researcher at Reform think tank at the time of contributing to the writing of the first chapter in this volume. His research focusses on applying quantitative methods to a range of policy issues – from the distribution effects of Social Care spending to the impact of contextualised admissions on widening participation in higher education.

Professor Tony Wall is Professor and Founder/Director of the International Thriving at Work Research Group at the University of Chester, where he leads numerous research and impact projects, Professional Doctorates and holds editorial positions with various international journals. He has three Santander International Research Excellence Awards, and he is a Visiting Scholar at Research Centres in the UK, Australia and the United States. His research and practice focus is on 'thriving' across multiple cultural and ecological contexts.

Professor Dianne Willcocks CBE, DL, is Emeritus Professor at York St John University, Honorary Doctor at Sheffield Hallam University and Honorary Fellow of Rose Bruford College. Formerly Vice Chancellor at York St John University, she is an advocate and practitioner for socially inclusive citizenship, promoting educational endeavour and opportunity that engages with the needs of modern communities. She is Vice Chair of the Joseph Rowntree Foundation and the York Teaching Hospital Foundation Trust.

1

ACCESS TO SUCCESS AND SOCIAL MOBILITY THROUGH HIGHER EDUCATION: A CURATE'S EGG?

Stuart Billingham

GLOBAL CONTEXTS

Increasing and widening access to lifelong learning, post-secondary and tertiary education has been, in one guise or another, a political issue for a very long time. In the UK, it stretches back as far as the immediate post-First World War concern with social and economic reconstruction (Burke & Jackson, 2007). Since then, there have been a very large number of government and other reports and initiatives about widening participation (WP).

Globally, efforts by many authorities have produced significant change. For example, a recent report by the United Nations Educational, Scientific and Cultural Organization

(UNESCO) (2017) notes that 'Worldwide there are DOUBLE the amount of students in higher education now than there were in 2000'.[1] Despite such apparent successes, these matters were included as one of the key Sustainable Development Goals agreed by all 193 members of the United Nations in September 2015.[2] As UNESCO (2017) puts it,

> *Target 4.3 states that, by 2030, countries should provide equal access for all women and men to affordable and quality technical, vocational and higher education, including university. Achieving this target will facilitate the achievement not only of SDG4 but also of all other SDGs. (p. 1)*

Access to post-secondary and higher education also sits within the core of WISE – the World Innovation Summit for Education – an 'international, multisectoral platform for creative thinking, debate and purposeful action' regarding education.[3] However, a recent attempt to draw a global map of access to post-secondary and tertiary education (Atherton, Dunmangane, & Whitty, 2016) found that,

> *Across the 23 OECD countries, a child's chances of participating in tertiary education are twice as high if at least one of their parents has completed upper secondary or post-secondary non-tertiary education. If one of their parents had a tertiary education, their chances of participating in it themselves are over four times as high. (pp. 22–23)*

---

1 See http://en.unesco.org/gem-report/gem-report-higher-education-policy-paper-social-media-resources

2 The SDGs came into force on 1 January 2016.

3 See http://www.wise-qatar.org

Whatever the limitations of the data on which these conclusions are based (and which are fully acknowledged in the study), such a picture supports the need for ongoing research, global debate and action. Graeme Atherton focusses on this, specifically, in the final chapter of the present volume. Clara Gwatirera examines government approaches to access in South Africa; Margaret Noble and Jessica Grant discuss access to tertiary education in rural and remote areas of New Zealand and Tasmania; and Bruria Schaedel considers aspects of diverse student experiences through a case study in Northern Israel. So, what is the essence of these debates?

Simply, it is about trying to understand, and then change, unfair and unequal patterns of who gets to study at a university (access); what happens to them once they are there (the student experience) and what happens to them once they leave (social mobility). Over the years, the terms of reference of this debate – what I will call its 'discourse' – have shifted significantly. This is arguably most easily illustrated in the UK, and on which I will now concentrate.

THE 'ACCESS' DEBATE

Throughout the 1960s, 1970s and even into the early 1980s, the primary focus was 'access'. Initially, this was as much about increasing the number of students in tertiary education as it was about widening the profile of the student population. Inevitably, however, those concerned to increase the university student population realised that this could only be achieved through widening its social and economic base.

Early concerns often focussed on access by 'adult learners', or 'mature' students, as they would later be called. 'Access Courses' sprang up in further education colleges, adult education centres and, later, in some university departments. They were designed to enable adult learners to return to study at a level, which would give them access to university, even though they did not have the standard 'A'-level entry qualification. And so, the 'Access movement' was born.

Such expansion of Higher Education (HE) was built upon a key principle (The Robbins Principle) enshrined in a seminal report, thus:

> *Throughout our Report we have assumed as an axiom that courses of higher education should be available for all those who are qualified by ability and attainment to pursue them and who wish to do so (Committee on Higher Education, 1963, p. 8).*

The idea of an 'Open University', developed by Labour Governments throughout the 1960s, was founded on this principle. The UK Open University opened its doors to its first students in 1971. From then until now, it has catered overwhelmingly for adult learners, studying part-time through distance learning.[4]

Later in this book, Liz Marr and John Butcher explore the challenges which policy-makers face with regard to part-time study for adult learners in the current political, economic and access policy climate in which the number of 'mature students' in higher education has fallen by over half since 2011 (Tuckett, 2018). From a different angle, Gerard Sharpling and Neil Murray consider the transformative effect on a university teacher's own pedagogy of studying part-time through distance-learning, whilst still teaching. The access discourse stresses the role of *outward-facing (outreach)* institutional strategies – explored here, for example, through the

---

4 It is interesting to note the long pedigree which distance learning has, because many people might easily believe it is a much more recent development given the media profile of Massive Open Online Courses.

case of Coventry University Scarborough Campus by Craig Gaskell and Ian Dunn.

THE WP DISCOURSE

The 'Robbins Principle' continued to influence access policy and practice for a long time and, in some ways, very much still does. This is despite the emergence of a 'new' discourse in the 1980s, which has largely dominated 'access' research, policy and practice ever since.

The WP discourse naturally maintains a concern with access, but goes on to focus more upon the *experience* of those students encouraged into university by access initiatives. This discourse focusses our attention, therefore, on *inward-facing* institutional policies and practices – for example, induction, student support, teaching and learning and retention – triggered by sustained sector-wide evidence of systematically skewed patterns of success at university.

Chris Millward, the new director for access and participation in the Office for Students (OfS) (see more in the following paragraphs), summarises the latest picture:

> *...black, Asian or disabled students and students from disadvantaged neighbourhoods are significantly less likely to succeed at university. The differences are stark: the proportion of students who get a first or 2:1 degree is 10 percentage points lower for students from the most disadvantaged backgrounds than for their wealthier peers, three points lower for those with a disability than for those without, and 22 and 11 points lower respectively for black and Asian students than for white students. (Millward, 2018)*

A key part of the debate about how to design, implement and evaluate policies to change this picture often raised the question: do we simply need better student-facing policies for *all* students, or specific ones targeted at 'WP students'?[5]

Thomas and Jones (2007) expressed it well, a decade ago,

> *...achieving more diverse patterns of participation depends not on 'normalising' students – i.e. slotting non-traditional entrants into traditional structures and processes. Rather, it is a matter of recognising different backgrounds, experiences and interests in order to develop more progressive, responsive forms of HE. (p. 5)*

Liz Thomas picks up this theme in the present volume, drawing on contemporary case study material as well as recent action research with thirteen UK Higher Education Institutions (HEIs) implementing change in 43 academic areas.

In some respects, Thomas and Jones (2007) were reflecting The National Committee of Inquiry into Higher Education – the Dearing Report (1997) – which famously extended the 'Robbins Principle' when it concluded that,

> *The future will require higher education in the UK to: encourage and enable all students – whether they demonstrate the highest intellectual potential or whether they have struggled to reach the threshold of higher education – to achieve beyond their expectations (para. 5).*

Stimulated by this report, the WP discourse gradually and progressively 'morphed' into one not just focussed on the

---

5 Though widely used among practitioners, this shorthand is strongly rejected by the author.

student experience in general, but more specifically on academic outcomes and social mobility: the language of access to success.

ACCESS TO SUCCESS: POLICY AND PRACTICE

A number of papers in the present volume examine the student experience, and student outcome, dimensions of the 'access to success' discourse. Helen May and Mark Jones, both of Advance HE,[6] examine evidence about what 'social capital' can contribute to student success; Siobhan Clay considers the experiences and future-oriented perspectives, of Black, Asian, Minority Ethnic and White students in a specialist Arts university; Nick Rowe and Simon Newton discuss an innovative approach to delivering higher educational learning opportunities to people who use mental health services; Tony Wall, Dwight Giles and Tim Stanton examine the history, and contemporary relevance to our field, of 'service learning' – a 30-year old education movement in the USA driven by goals of social justice and community engagement; and Nik Miller considers what should be done to narrow the gap in graduate outcomes when measured by socio-economic background.

The recent evolution of the WP discourse reflects, and in turn has itself helped to shape, a number of important policy initiatives. Here are just three, which I consider to be of particular policy and practitioner significance over the last decade and going forward:

---

6 From March 2018, Advance HE is the name given to the new organisation formed through the merger of the Higher Education Academy (HEA), the Equality Challenge Unit, and the Leadership Foundation for Higher Education. Its new structure takes effect in August 2018.

- The introduction in 2000 of the HEA National Teaching
  Fellowship (NTF) award: a competitive process involving
  teachers being nominated by their institution for
  demonstrating outstanding impact on student outcomes
  and the teaching profession. If successful, the individual
  receives the much sought-after NTF title with the
  requirement to support enhancement of teaching and
  learning in their university and beyond. According to the
  HEA, there are currently over 815 NTFs. In 2016, the
  HEA introduced a sister award 'Collaborative Award for
  Teaching Excellence', aimed at recognising the impact of
  teamwork in delivering student success.

- In 2005, the National Student Survey (NSS), which asks
  final year undergraduate students about key aspects of
  their learning experience and publishes a league table
  of the results. The intention is for such results to help
  enhance the quality of student learning. In my experience
  of the first few years following its introduction, the
  NSS certainly focussed the collective mind of university
  senior management on the student experience and how
  to improve it where necessary. However, the NSS has not
  been without its critics with concerns about its publication
  in a league table, as well as significant and fundamental
  questions around its methodology and epistemology.
  Despite my experience of the way it galvanised senior
  managers and the positive change agenda which followed,
  I share those concerns – the nub of which is summarised
  succinctly by Scott et al. (2014),

  > *student experiences need to be understood in
  > context, and not through disconnected and de-
  > contextualised technologies, such as the various
  > types of student satisfaction surveys currently in
  > use. (p. 1)*

- The creation of the new OfS established by the Higher Education and Research Act, 2017. Amongst many other powers, it arranges for assessing the quality of teaching in universities through the new Teaching Excellence Framework (TEF). The first TEF results were published in June 2017.[7]

Interestingly – at least in terms of the argument being developed in this Introduction – the Department for Education changed the name of this exercise to the 'Teaching Excellence and Student Outcomes Framework' in October 2017. However, it has retained the 'TEF' acronym rather than the clumsier, though more accurate, 'TEaSOF' – and for possibly sensible media-related reasons.

The Office for Fair Access (OFFA) was merged into the new OfS, with a new director for access and participation, with effect from April 2018. New style, and re-named, Access and Participation Plans will be part of the registration requirements for 'Approved' (i.e. fee-capped) institutions.[8] Governing bodies are now also required to publish information on the 'fairness of their admissions'.

ACCESS TO SUCCESS: FEES AND REGULATION

The language now used routinely by government to describe the function of the OfS is that of 'regulator' – a shift in the dominant political discourse regarding university education, which has been progressively taking place for nearly

---

7 For a comprehensive and critical discussion of the Teaching Excellence initiative, see French and O'Leary (2017).

8 For a useful guide to the powers and responsibilities of the OfS, see https://wonkhe.com/blogs/a-beginners-guide-to-the-office-for-students/.

two decades. This discourse creates significant tensions and
clashes between the language and conceptualisation of WP
circulating in the corridors of Westminster and Whitehall and
those amongst practitioners in institutions. Within this context, it is perhaps unsurprising that the question of student
tuition fees will almost certainly be seen as the defining WP
issue of the present decade.

The Browne Report (2010) effectively set the stage for current[9] student tuition fee arrangements in UK higher education –
though it had a difficult birth and an equally challenging
early infancy. Whilst it made a large number of recommendations about the funding of higher education, it was the *principle* of having no 'cap' on tuition charges that universities levy
on students, that is the most controversial. Browne (and subsequent amendments) linked the new tuition fee regime to a HE
provider's plans to attract and support students from 'disadvantaged backgrounds' as described in their Access Agreement
with OFFA.[10] Since then, the issue of tuition fees has never been
far from the headlines.

In addition, as if to reinforce the point, the Prime Minister
launched a new 'Review of Post-18 Education and Funding' in
February 2018. The Review has a very broad remit[11] which,
some might say, reads as if it is trying to be all things to all people. Either way, it includes some very familiar policy rhetoric. It
will consider how to ensure that the post-18 education system

- is accessible to all,

- can be supported by a value for money funding regime,
  which works for students and taxpayers,

---

9 June 2018.

10 From April 2018, Access and Participation Plans are submitted to the OfS.

11 See https://www.gov.uk/government/uploads/system/uploads/attach-
   ment_data/file/682348/Post_18_review_-_ToR.pdf.

- incentivises choice and competition across the sector and

- will develop the skills needed as a country.

However, when the Review Panel publishes its interim report (before the Review is concluded in early 2019), it is likely that the headlines will be grabbed by two constraints under which it has worked: there must be no cap on student numbers in post-18 education and students should contribute to the cost of their studies.

ACCESS TO SUCCESS: SOCIAL MOBILITY

In 2011, the government firmly hitched all questions about WP to the social mobility bandwagon,

> *In a fair society what counts is not the school you went to or the jobs your parents did, but your ability and your ambition. In other words, fairness is about social mobility. (H.M. Government, 2011, p. 11)*

Yet, the shift to making social mobility central to WP policy really began at the start of the 1980s, with the emergence of a new consensus about what social mobility meant (Goldthorpe, 2012). From this time on, all major political parties seem agreed that increasing the rates of *relative*[12] social mobility must be a key priority of WP (and indeed other) policies.

Importantly, successive governments have believed that this goal will only be achieved if universities and other HE providers change, in deep and fundamental ways, as exempli-

---

12 *Relative social mobility* refers to the *chances* of individuals from different social class origins moving into different class destinations.

fied in this extract from a Letter of Guidance to the Director for Fair Access from the Secretary of State:

> *Real, lasting, progress can only be made by achieving cultural change throughout higher education institutions (BIS, 2016, para. 3.8, p. 4).*

This positioning had within it a much sharper focus on access to high tariff (or 'elite') institutions and, chiefly through them, to the professions. As Simon Hughes had said in 2011,

> *And I underline that there are particular courses which need particular attention if we are to widen access: medicine, dentistry, veterinary science, and architecture, for example. (p. 5)*

This major new focus of WP policy is explored in the present volume through significant original research by Emilie Sundorph, Danail Vasilev and Louis Coiffait in our next chapter, and is further examined later by Nik Miller.

AN ALTERNATIVE DISCOURSE?

Whilst the *dominant* WP discourse has gradually and progressively developed into one centred on student outcomes measured by social mobility – within a framework of ever-increasing regulation – there has been a parallel or even subterranean discourse: that of 'equality, diversity and inclusion' which, in my experience, reflects the aims and aspirations of many WP 'academic-practitioners'.

However, it would be wholly inaccurate to say that this way of conceptualising the objectives of WP has only very recently been used with regard to student-facing HE policies. Shaw et al. (2008) put it like this,

> *Over the last fifteen years, a 'diversity discourse' has*
> *emerged in the USA ... and the UK ... which claims*
> *to recognise broader dimensions of inequality*
> *than those within the scope of standard equal*
> *opportunities policies. (p. 31)*

Importantly, they go on to note how this 'diversity discourse' challenges the way the WP discourse can promote a deficit view, or even 'victim-blaming' (Billingham, 2006), of the populations or groups they serve.

The origins of this 'diversity discourse' in UK education lay with concerns about the ethnic, gender, sexuality, age and disability profiles of *staff* in universities and colleges. The discourse now embraces institutional policy objectives relating to both staff and students. However, in the past, it rarely informed policies concerned specifically with WP. More recently, this discourse has begun to challenge the dominant WP policy framework by highlighting the needs of populations historically marginalised or completely ignored within the WP discourse, such as students leaving local authority care, estranged students[13] and those using mental health services.[14] In addition, the diversity discourse, challenging though it can be to implement,[15] not only figures within the policies of many HEIs but also, for example, at the Higher Education Funding Council for England HEFCE.[16]

Given all this, and that the UK signed-up to SDG4 'on inclusive and equitable quality education' (UNESCO, 2017), the discourse of equity, diversity and inclusion often struggles to find its way into *national* policy statements about WP.

---

13 See http://standalone.org.uk/wpcontent/uploads/2013/08/StandAlone
     UNITEfoundation.pdf.

14 See the Chapter in this volume by Nick Rowe and Simon Newton.

15 See https://www.theguardian.com/higher-education-network/2017/
     may/31/a-clash-of-personalities-why-universities-mustnt-ignore-race.

16 See, for example, http://www.hefce.ac.uk/workprovide/ed/.

Most recently, however, such policy objectives do feature in the Guidance to Institutions from the OfS about writing their Access and Participation Plans 2019–2020, published in February 2018.[17] However, the reference seems mostly concerned with protected characteristics rather than with the broader diversity discourse to which this chapter is referring.

CONCLUDING COMMENTS

As I have tried to demonstrate in this *very* brief introductory overview of the discourses of 'access to success', the *dominant* WP discourse is not now just about who gets in to HE, nor only their experience once there. It is also centrally about chances for individual social mobility, especially as measured by access to the most selective universities and professions. At a systemic level, it is also about ever-tighter government regulation to achieve this goal – as shown powerfully through the remit of the OfS and the new Review of Post-18 Education and Funding. So, where do we stand now?

There has been good progress with WP in some countries; in parts of some countries; and for some groups in some countries. UK HE providers have explicit equity, diversity and inclusion policies and their Access and Participation Plans – and the supporting WP policies – whilst generally not built explicitly around these concepts are at least expected to refer to them.

However, student-facing WP statements often still reflect the dominant WP discourse of the pre-OfS era: especially of targeted outreach, academic achievement, progression, and outcomes. Whilst these foci are, in my experience, endorsed by WP practitioners and institutional leaders, many would much prefer

---

17   See https://www.officeforstudents.org.uk/publications/regulatory-notice-1-guidance-on-access-and-participa tion-plans-for-2019-20/.

a discourse, which is *centred* around the concepts of equality/
equity, diversity and inclusion, and is expressed through a
corresponding discourse.

At the heart of the battle between the current dominant
WP discourse and such alternative ones, lies the question of
*who controls how universities and other HEIs approach this
agenda.*

These critical questions of power and authority on what is
good WP strategy and implementation policy and what is not
are signalled by the subtitle to this book – A Curate's Egg.[18]
The following chapters explore these questions through
innovative research, practice and unique critical-analytical
reflections.

REFERENCES

Atherton, G., Dunmangane, C., & Whitty, G. (2016).
*Charting equity in higher education: Drawing the global
access map.* London: Pearson.

Billingham, S. (2006). Long live widening participation:
An integrated strategy for sustainability. Paper presented
at the 15th European Access Network Annual Conference,
Thessaloniki, EAN.

18 'A Curate's Egg' means 'a thing that is partly good and partly bad'. It
   stems from a cartoon published in the satirical UK magazine *Punch* in
   1895, which depicted a Curate who, given a stale egg at the Bishop's table,
   assures his host that 'parts of it are excellent'. The cartoon is a metaphor
   for describing things which are partly good and partly not, but especially
   how power relations affect the way we describe and deal with them.

BIS. (2016). Letter of Guidance from the Secretary of State for Business, Innovation and Skills and the Minister of State for Universities and Science to the Director for Fair Access. Retrieved from https://www.offa.org.uk/wp-content/uploads/2016/02/11-02-2016-OFFA-Guidance.pdf

Burke, P. J., & Jackson, S. (2007). *Reconceptualising lifelong learning: Feminist interventions*. Abingdon: Routledge.

Committee on Higher Education. (1963). *Higher education: Report of the Committee Appointed the Prime Minister under the Chairmanship of Lord Robbins, 1961–1963, (The Robbins Report), Cmnd. 2154*. London: HMSO.

Dearing, R. (1997). *Higher education in the learning society. (The Dearing Report)*. London: National Committee of Inquiry into Higher Education.

French, A., & O'Leary, M. (Eds.). (2017). *Teaching excellence in higher education: Challenges, changes and the teaching excellence framework*. Bingley: Emerald Publishing.

Goldthorpe, J. H. (2012). *Understanding – and misunderstanding – Social mobility in Britain: The entry of the Economists, the confusion of politicians and the limits of educational policy*. Barnett Papers in Social Research, Department of Social Policy and Intervention, University of Oxford.

Government, H. M. (2011). *Opening doors, breaking barriers: A strategy for social mobility*. London: HMSO.

Hughes, S. (2011). *Report to the Prime Minister and Deputy Prime Minister from the Advocate for Access to Education, (The Hughes Report)*. London: Cabinet Office.

Millward, C. (2018, April 9) 'Wealthy, white students still do best at university. We must close the gap', Higher Education Network. *The Guardian*. London. Retrieved from https://www.theguardian.com/higher-education-network/2018/

apr/09/wealthy-white-students-still-do-best-at-university-we-must-close-the-gap

Scott D., Hughes. G., Evans. C., Burke, P. J., Walter. C., & Watson, D. (2014). *Learning transitions in higher education.* Basingstoke: Palgrave Macmillan.

Shaw, J., Brain, K., Bridger, K., Foreman, J., & Reid, I. (2008). Student diversity = Student success. In F. Ferrier & M. Heagney (Eds.), *Higher education in diverse communities: Global perspectives, local initiatives.* London: EAN.

Thomas, L., & Jones, R. (2007). Embedding employability in the context of widening participation. In Yorke, M., (Ed) *Learning and Employability*, Series Two. York: HEA

Tuckett, A. (2018, April 19). 'The world of work is changing. We need more adult education, not less', Higher Education Network. *The Guardian*. Retrieved from https://www. theguardian.com/higher-education-network/2018/apr/19/the-world-of-work-is-changing-we-need-more-adult-education-not-less

UNESCO. (2017, April). *Six ways to ensure higher education leaves no one behind*. Global Monitoring Report (Policy Paper 30). Paris: UNESCO.

SECTION A

ASPECTS OF THE CONTEMPORARY ACCESS DEBATE

2

ACCESS TO THE ELITE

*Emilie Sundorph, Danail Vasilev and
Louis Coiffait*

ABSTRACT

*It is argued by many that one of the keys to social
mobility lies in widening access to institutions, which
educate most of the 'elite'. In England, around 30 of the
most highly selective universities are responsible for the
higher education of a large proportion of those ending
up in the most well-paid and powerful positions. These
institutions have historically recruited most of their
students from middle- or upper-class backgrounds,
and still struggle to create more diverse student bodies.
Investments in (so-called) widening participation (WP)
have increased significantly, and institutions widely
advertise their commitment to diversity. Still, increasing
the proportion of students from lower socio-economic
backgrounds is progressing incredibly slowly.*

This chapter investigates how highly selective universities can best be held to account for their contribution to social mobility. It explores the direction of WP spending and the case for implementing a framework ensuring that institutions seek to achieve value for money. It ranks the progress of the most selective universities, and by investigating the approach taken at the most successful one, the LSE recommends a greater focus on contextualised admissions.

Keywords: Access; social mobility; selective universities; contextualised admissions

INTRODUCTION

The UK is struggling to increase social mobility. Against comparable countries, it has one of the strongest links between individual earnings and parental income (Isaacs, 2017), and more than half of people aged from 18 to 24 believe that where you end up in society is mainly determined by your background (Social Mobility Commission, 2017).

Access to 'elite' universities has become a symbol of differences in opportunity experienced by people from different social backgrounds.[1] Every year, intakes are scrutinised for the proportion of disadvantaged students, and not with great outcomes. In 2016, the most advantaged quintile of young people were almost 11 times more likely to gain access to a high UCAS tariff institution than the most disadvantaged (UCAS Analysis and Research, 2016).

---

1 'Elite' universities here refer to UCAS high-tariff universities; i.e. those with the most selective admission criteria.

Their dominance in educating the most powerful is also highlighted – in 2016, around 90% of senior civil servants attended a Sutton Trust 'Top 30 University', and almost a third of FTSE 100 CEOs attended Oxford or Cambridge universities (Kirby, 2016).[2]

HE institutions (HEIs) are aware that improvements are needed.

Across the sector, more than £1 billion was spent on widening participation (WP) activities in 2015–2016 (Office for Fair Access (OFFA), 2017b). Despite only making up around 20% of the universities which submit Access Agreements to the OFFA – see below – high-tariff institutions account for more than 40% of HEI spend on WP (OFFA, 2017a). Given the limited progress in this area, it is crucial that these institutions understand how to achieve value for money.

Most university WP spending comes from fee income, and it could be argued, therefore, that universities are free to spend it as they see fit. However, the student loan system is heavily subsidised by the state (Crawford, 2014), and universities should be held accountable for spending resources in the most productive way like other public services.

This chapter is focussed on identifying ways in which highly selective universities can increase access for young disadvantaged students, and to improve the accountability system for doing so successfully. More than 15 years ago, a report by the Select Committee on Education and Employment highlighted the importance of a 'more representative social mix in admissions to high status research-intensive universities, many of whose graduates go on to hold positions of power in business, industry, the professions and in politics'

---

2 The Sutton Top 30 list includes most Russell Group universities and other highly selective institutions.

(House of Commons, 2001, para. 74). Not enough progress has been made since then.

Efforts to Date

Only 3.6% of 18 year olds from low-participation areas entered high-tariff institutions in 2016–2017, as opposed to 21.3% of those from the highest participation areas (UCAS Analysis and Research, 2016).[3]

The intake of disadvantaged students as a proportion of all entrants to English universities is shown in Fig. 1. Increases in participation have largely been driven by the creation of additional places at mid- and lower-tariff institutions. These universities have seen a decrease in applicants recently (UCAS Analysis and Research, 2017), and continue to have stronger incentives than high-tariff institutions to engage with schools and students from low-participation areas.

Since the 2004 Higher Education Act, English HEIs have been required to submit Access Agreements for approval by OFFA, outlining how they intend to increase access for disadvantaged and under-represented groups. The plans must be approved for HEIs to charge fees beyond the 'basic amount' of £6,165, up to £9,250 (HEFCE, 2015A).

In addition to the spending monitored by OFFA, funding is also allocated centrally by HEFCE. The HEFCE funding targeted at disadvantaged students peaked at £400 million in 2016–2017, but is planned to fall by up to half by 2019–2020

---

3 Low-participation areas are those where there is the lowest quintile of higher education participation of young people; the highest participation areas are in the top quintile. These are defined by the Higher Education Statistics Agency (HESA).

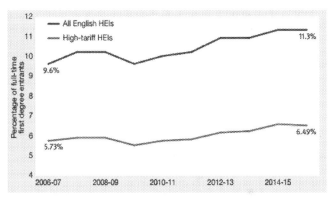

Fig. 1. Reform Calculations based on *Higher Education Statistics Agency* (HESA) Performance Indicators.

(Bolton, 2017).[4] HEIs may also have access to some external and charitable funds for their WP work.

Universities report annually in their Access Agreements what proportion of fee income will be dedicated to five WP categories; 'access', 'student success', 'progression', 'hardship' and 'financial support'.[5] The resources allocated to WP have been rising steadily, totalling Agreement spending of £725 million in 2015–2016 (OFFA, 2017c). The increase is greater at high-tariff institutions, who spent 45% more per enrolled student than other universities in 2015–2016.

In total, including HEFCE allocations and external funds, £232 million was spent on the 'access' category in 2015–2016 (OFFA, 2017c). Of this, £184.3 million came from fee income. As Access Agreement spending is the most consistently report-ed at an institutional level and most comparable over the past five years, it is the measure used in the present research.

---

4   Though it is possible, this might be changed by the Review of Post-18 Education and Funding announced by the Government in February 2018.

5   These categories have been in place since 2015–2016, with previous headings slightly different.

Slow Progress

Despite significant investment, high-tariff universities have made almost no progress. Table 1 ranks high-tariff HEIs based on their record in increasing access for students from low-participation areas. The table considers institutions' proportional intake, but performance against a benchmark set by Higher Education Statistics Agency (HESA) is also included. The benchmark is an estimate of the proportion of disadvantaged students that a HEI should be able to recruit, given its selectiveness and subject mix.[6]

From 2011–2012 to 2015–2016, the university which progressed most, in terms of accepting a greater proportion of disadvantaged students, was LSE. Of the 29 universities, 25 made some progress in terms of proportional intakes. Some universities accepted a relatively high proportion in 2011, leaving little space for improvement. For example, Lancaster University may not have increased its proportion of disadvantaged students by much; however, over the four years, it has consistently beaten its benchmark, as shown in the second column. Only five others have on average been above their benchmarks.

The measure of disadvantage used by HEFCE, based on HE participation rates in the area of the student's family home, has been criticised, especially by urban universities who recruit students from neighbourhoods where the most and least advantaged often live side by side. UCAS has created an alternative 'multiple equality measure' to take into account individual-level features, including family income (UCAS, 2016). Almost 64 per cent of young people in the lowest MEM quintile are from POLAR3 quintile 1 areas. More

---

6   The methodology used to construct the benchmarks can be found in
    HESA (2017) 'Benchmarks (Applicable to Tables T1 to T3, T7 and E1)'.

than 96 per cent of POLAR3 quintile 1 students are in one of the two lowest MEM quintiles. Whilst imperfect, this suggests that measures of low-participation neighbourhoods capture most of the disadvantaged students.

Impact of Spending

Outreach spending levels are spread across universities with different performances. Paradoxically, perhaps, and as seen in Table 1, spending the most appears to correlate with lower performance.

However, a simple look at the lack of a positive correlation between spending level and performance has limitations: some universities travel further to reach WP applicants and some are encouraged to spend more due to poor historical WP performance. Still, the differences in spending and apparent absence of a positive link to performance suggests resources are not providing the best value for money that many might expect them to.

Universities are encouraged to focus greater resources on raising attainment at younger ages, on the basis that it has a higher rate of return (OFFA, 2016). Any efforts to increase impact should be applauded, but most of the tangible targets which institutions have been encouraged to set relate only to their own yearly intake, which is less likely to be affected by early investment.

There is a need for closer monitoring of the age groups towards which resources are directed, and a clarification of the desired outcomes. If a large part of 'access' resources goes to pupils in a primary or secondary school, with the general aim of supporting social mobility, the measure of success should be different, as should the evaluation of value for money. Increasing take-up of tools such as the Higher Education Access Tracker (2017), a non-profit service monitoring

Table 1. Proportional intake of disadvantaged students at English universities

University	Average annual increase in the proportion of dis-advantaged students 2011-12 to 2015-16	Average distance from HESA benchmark 2011-12 to 2015-16 (percentage points)	Change in distance from HESA benchmark 2011-12 to 2015-16 (percentage points)	Per-student expenditure across all entrants (5-year average)
LSE	1.13	−0.54	4.50	£634
University of York	0.63	−0.10	0.90	£437
University of East Anglia	0.43	−0.38	0.60	£536
University of Leeds	0.40	0.32	0.70	£246
The University of Manchester	0.40	0.52	0.70	£269
University of Bristol	0.35	−2.26	1.10	£542
The University of Sheffield	0.30	0.80	0.40	£612
University of Southampton	0.28	−0.62	−0.60	£274
Loughborough University	0.23	−2.00	−0.10	£308
University of Leicester	0.18	−0.68	−1.40	£474
Lancaster University	0.18	1.44	−1.30	£319
University of Birmingham	0.15	−0.78	−0.20	£343
King's College London	0.15	−2.36	−0.60	£450

University of Cambridge	0.15	-1.42	0.50	£538
University of Liverpool	0.15	1.10	-0.80	£253
SOAS	0.13	-4.44	-1.60	£506
University of Nottingham	0.13	-1.02	-0.80	£380
University of Bath	0.10	-1.38	0.00	£429
University of Surrey	0.08	-1.82	-1.40	£198
Imperial College London	0.08	-1.10	0.00	£346
Royal Holloway, UoL	0.08	-3.34	-1.20	£367
University of Oxford	0.05	-1.82	0.10	£1,053
Durham University	0.05	-1.02	-0.10	£956
Newcastle University	0.03	0.56	-1.10	£820
Queen Mary UoL*	0.01	-3.88	-0.50	£104
The University of Warwick	0.00	-0.86	-0.40	£622
University College London	-0.08	-1.90	-1.00	£692
University of Exeter	-0.13	-2.02	-1.30	£319
St George's, UoL	-0.58	-2.56	-2.90	£763

Upper quartile   Lower quartile

Sources: Reform calculations based on HESA performance indicators and OFFA monitoring outcomes. Expenditure refers to spending on the 'access' category in access agreements, or what was previously reported under 'outreach.'

Note: Figures for Queen Mary University of London are only available from 2012 onwards, hence figures are based on the period 2012-13 to 2015-16 the outcomes of students taking part in WP activities, could prove helpful in setting such outcome measures.

Focussing on Admissions

Given the uncertainty of impact when working with younger children, universities will have to consider other approaches alongside such efforts. The one tool they have full control over is admissions policy, with many universities starting to introduce so-called 'contextualised admissions', where an applicant's achievements are considered against the backdrop of their social background.

In 2015, the 29 most selective universities would collectively have had to admit 3,470 more disadvantaged students to reach their HESA benchmark (HESA, 2017). During interviews for this research, admissions policy was repeatedly highlighted as a necessary lever to improve, with one WP professional stating 'no university that claims to be serious about WP can ignore contextualised admissions'.

Many of these universities have introduced some form of contextualised admissions since 2006. However, because a group of HEIs do not contextualise, an estimation of the total effect of contextualisation can only be made using HESA data and a synthetic control method.[7] Fig. 2. summarises the findings from this analysis[8].

These data compare a university, which has introduced contextualised admissions, LSE, to a constructed weighted average of universities, which resemble LSE in terms of certain observable characteristics, but have not introduced contextualised

---

7   As applied in Abadie, Diamond, and Hainmueller (2010).
8   The methodology, data and detailed findings are summarised in Sundorph, Danail, and Coiffait (2017).

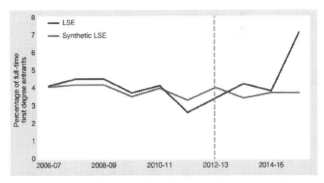

Fig. 2.   Disadvantaged Student Intake at LSE and at
the Synthetic Control Group. Calculations based on HESA
performance indicators and OFFA access agreements.

admissions.[9] The synthetic control group tracks LSE closely
in terms of the proportion of disadvantaged students prior to
2012 – when LSE introduced contextual admissions.

After 2012, the trend in the control group is an estimate of
what would have happened at LSE if contextual admissions
had **not** been introduced. The gap between the lines representing LSE and the synthetic control group is an estimate
of the causal effect of contextualised admissions. According
to LSE, this was the only significant change to their admissions practices in this period, although it was accompanied by
continuous evaluations of practices.

The analysis suggests LSE's contextualised admissions
scheme is successful, increasing the proportion of WP students by an average 0.93 percentage points per year from
2011–2012 to 2015–2016. The biggest increase occurred in

---

9   Based on access agreements, universities that only apply contextual
     admissions in cases of verified extenuating circumstances are not
     included. Observable characteristics included are HESA benchmarks and
     Access Agreement expenditure.

2015–2016, where the estimated effect of the policy was an increase of 3.41 percentage points.

If the other 29 high-tariff institutions emulated the effect of LSE's approach in 2015–2016, 3,552 more WP students would enrol each year. The effect would depend, of course, on the availability of suitable WP applicants, as universities could be competing for the same disadvantaged students.[10]

The evidence so far suggests that contextualised admissions have not had the negative impact on academic standards, which some predict. Although there is limited published research available on contextualised admission schemes, indications are positive. St. George's Medical School has run its Adjusted Criteria scheme since 2002, where students with A-level results 60% above their school's average (at low-performing schools) are guaranteed interviews. Between 2002 and 2008, the programme accounted for about 7% of intakes, and in first-year exams its participants scored only 0.61 percentage points lower than the rest (The Sutton Trust, 2009).

Conclusion

Despite stated commitments to diversity and fair access, a resistance to systematic contextual admissions persists. Even when institutions successfully implement contextual information, there is reluctance to share methods, lessons learned and outcomes. Interviewees in the present research spoke of a need to preserve a 'safe space' to work on contextual methods and avoid charges of unequal treatment. Given slow pro-

---

10 The total 3,552 is therefore an upper boundary to the increase in disadvantaged students gaining access through this method of contextualisation.

gress, however, and the detrimental effect on access to success and social mobility, this should not be tolerated. Considering applicants in context is not 'social engineering', merely a step towards a fairer and more socially mobile society.

REFERENCES

Abadie, A., Diamond, A., & Hainmueller, J. (2010). Synthetic control methods for comparative case studies: Estimating the effect of California's tobacco control program. *Journal of the American Statistical Association*, *105*, 493–505.

Bolton, P. (2017). *Higher education funding in England*. London: House of Commons Library.

Britton, J., Dearden, L., Shephard, N., & Vignoles, A. (2016). *How English domiciled graduate earnings vary with gender, institution attended, subject and socio-economic background*. London: The Institute for Fiscal Studies.

Crawford, C. (2014). *Estimating the public cost of student loans*. London: The Institute for Fiscal Studies.

HEFCE. (2015). Guidance on Tuition Fee Regulations. Retrieved from http://www.hefce.ac.uk/funding/fees/#note1

Higher Education Access Tracker. (2017). What is HEAT & Who are Our Members? Retrieved from http://heat.ac.uk/what-is-heat/

Higher Education Statistics Agency (HESA). (2017). Table T1a: Participation of Under-Represented Groups in Higher Education: UK Domiciled Young Full-Time First Degree Entrants 2015/16. Retrieved from https://www.hesa.ac.uk/data-and-analysis/performance-indicators/releases/2015-16-widening-participation.

House of Commons. (2001). *Select committee on education and employment (2001). Higher education: Access, fourth report of session 2000–2001*. London: The Stationery Office.

Isaacs, J. B. (2016). International comparisons of economic mobility. In J. B. Isaacs, I. V. Sawhill, & R. Haskins (Eds.), *Getting ahead or losing ground: Economic mobility in America*. Washington, DC: The Brookings Institution.

Kirby, P. (2016). *Leading people 2016: The educational background of the UK professional elite*. London: The Sutton Trust.

Office for Fair Access (OFFA). (2016). *Strategic guidance: Developing your 2017–18 access agreement*. Bristol: OFFA.

Office for Fair Access (OFFA). (2017). *Outcomes of access agreement monitoring for 2015–16*. Bristol: OFFA.

Social Mobility Commission. (2017). *Social mobility barometer: Public attitudes to social mobility in the UK*. London: Social Mobility Commission.

Sundorph, E., Vasilev, D. & Coiffait, L. (2017). *Joining the elite: How top universities can enhance social mobility*. London: Reform.

The Sutton Trust. (2009). *Innovative university admissions worldwide: A percent scheme for the UK?* London: The Sutton Trust.

UCAS. (2016). Equality and Entry Rates Data Explorer. Retrieved from https://www.ucas.com/corporate/data-and-analysis/ucas-undergraduate-releases/equality-and-entry-rates-data-explorer

UCAS Analysis and Research. (2016). *End of cycle report 2016*. Cheltenham: UCAS.

3

ACCESS TO HIGHER EDUCATION IN SOUTH AFRICA

Clara Gwatirera

ABSTRACT

Nelson Mandela once argued that 'education is the most powerful weapon, which you can use to change the world'. This sentiment is echoed by governments and citizens across the world. Education can help us to better understand the world around us and our place in it, equipping us to push for positive social, economic and political changes.

Calls for accessible Higher Education (HE) in South (and the rest of) Africa make perfect sense: a university degree is a passport to a better life for those who have it. For example, the unemployment rate for those with a university degree is significantly lower than for those without. In addition, university campuses offer more than just taught knowledge: they are a place where young people build networks, relationships and values (see, e.g. May & Jones in this volume, Chapter 5). They are where the future business, political and intellectual leaders of a country are forged.

Africa, generally, is faced with numerous serious challenges regarding access to HE, and this chapter explores some of the key ones with particular reference to South Africa.

Keywords: South Africa; access; quality; higher; education; government strategy

BACKGROUND INFORMATION ON ACCESS TO HIGHER EDUCATION IN SOUTH AFRICA

In his speech to American students at Wakefield High School in Arlington, Virginia (7 September 2009), President Barak Obama said, 'Higher education cannot be a luxury reserved just for a privileged few. It is an economic necessity for every family, and every family should be able to afford it'.

However, over the years, the cost of education generally in South Africa has grown to unaffordable rates; the quality remains poor and the literacy levels remain low.

> *In South Africa, social inequalities were entrenched and reflected in all spheres of social life as a product of the systemic exclusion of blacks and women under colonialism and apartheid. The higher education system was no different. Political and socio-economic discrimination, inequalities of class, race, gender, and of an institutional and spatial nature profoundly shaped, and continue to shape, South African Higher Education. (Badat, 2010, p. 4)*

Nevertheless, under democratic leadership since 1994, South Africa has undergone radical reforms of higher education (HE). Whilst challenges remain, there is a noticeable progress in the levels of access due to policy changes designed post-1994 to support mass HE. A wide array of transformation-oriented initiatives, seeking to effect institutional change, have included, such as:

- the definition of the purposes and goals of HE;

- extensive policy research, policy formulation, adoption and implementation in the areas of governance, funding, academic structure and programmes, and quality assurance;

- the enactment of new laws and regulations; and

- major restructuring and reconfiguration of the higher education institutional (HEI) landscape (Badat, 2010, pp. 4–5).

All informed by the National Commission on Higher Education of 1996 and the White Paper on Higher Education of 1997.

The Higher Education Act of 1997 was the first post-1994 fundamental policy initiative designed to ensure regulated transformation of institutions of higher learning. The Act was designed with the main intention of ensuring access to HE for more students from previously disadvantaged communities and to increase employment opportunities.

In line with promoting access, the government introduced the National Student Financial Aid Scheme (NSFAS) targeting poor students (Cele, 2014). The fund has had a fundamentally positive effect on access. Moreover, the South Africa Constitution of 1996 considers education a right, rather than a privilege (Bill of Rights). Whilst student access to HE in

South Africa is noted in a positive light, success still faces serious challenges. In response, many initiatives have been introduced in institutions and supported by the State.

The post-secondary education and training system in South Africa consists of public entities, which include the following:

- Council on Higher Education (CHE);

- NSFAS;

- Quality Council for Trades and Occupations;

- South African Qualifications Authority;

- National Skills Fund (NSF);

- Sector Education and Training Authorities;

- Universities, Technical and Vocational Education and Training (TVET) Colleges, the Community Colleges; and

- Registered private HEI.

Universities South Africa is a non-statutory membership organisation of Principals of South Africa's universities. The International Education Association of South Africa is a non-statutory membership organisation of International Office Directors and staff in South Africa's universities. According to the Draft Policy Framework for the Internationalisation of South African HE (2017), there are 26 universities classified into three types: 11 'traditional' universities, nine 'comprehensive' universities and six universities of technology. Three universities are relatively new, having been established during 2013–2014. There was a total of 73,859 international students (7.5% of the total student population of approximately 11.8 million) enrolled in the public HEIs (compared to 46,687 international students in 2002). Of the international students, 73% were from the South African Development Community countries,

16% from other African countries and 9% from the rest of the word (Department of Higher Education and Training, 2017).

Quality of Education in South Africa

The question of whether South Africa has made advances by making HE available and accessible since 1994 could get a resounding 'yes' when considering the growth in the number of students enrolled in South African HEIs including TVET colleges, community colleges and universities. The participation rate in HE for youth in the 20–24 age group increased from 17% in 2011 to 19.5% in 2013, against the 20% target set for 10 to 15 years by the National Plan for Higher Education (NPHE) in 2001(CHE, 2013). However, improvement in the quality of education has been very slow. The former Minister of Science and Technology,[1] Naledi Pandor said,

> *Access to education has opened up since 1994, but the government has been less successful at improving the quality of education pupils receive. In particular, South African government have not been able to improve the science and maths teaching in schools, and that has created a bottleneck in the expansion of the university system, and unemployment for many young people. (Pandor, 2015)*

CHALLENGES OF ACQUIRING HE IN SOUTH AFRICA

The #Fees-Must-Fall student protests in South Africa have highlighted the many challenges facing HE in South Africa.

---

1 Pandor became the Minister of Higher Education and Training in February 2018.

The protest started as a response to the announcement of a 10.5% University fees increase in October 2015 (Herschkowitz, 2017).

Although the focus of the protests was on a rise in fees, a number of factors formed the background to the protests, including:

- a lack of funding for poorer students to attend university;

- high incomes for university administrators;

- a real terms decline in government funding for HE; and

- lack of social transformation,

in order to broader socio-economic and racial inequality issues.

Government Funding

HE funding is the tip of an iceberg representing the challenges faced generally by education. Government budgeting for education has been, in most cases, too small to cater for scholarships and loans offered to students who meet the criteria; facilities such as properly equipped libraries and laboratories; sound university information systems; easy access to registration and conducive learning environments.

South Africa's spending on universities is comparatively low by world standards. In 2011, the state budget for universities, including funding for the NSFAS, as a percentage of gross domestic product (GDP) was 0.75%, just less than Africa as a whole (0.78%). The budget for the 2015–2016 fiscal year was 0.72% of GDP, lower than it was in 2011. This is also significantly lower when compared with the 2011 figures of African countries (0.78%), Organisation for Economic Co-operation and Development countries (1.21%) and the rest of the world (0.84%) (Nxasana, 2016).

Once the government does not act to show its support through budgetary allocation for education over all, the crises – which most often are strike actions by either teachers and/or students – begin to take shape. This even sets back international support and cooperation. Prolonged underfunding of HE amidst rising costs has led institutions to raise fees markedly every year, rapidly outpacing inflation. Management cultures have changed significantly to focus on economic and compliance imperatives.

> *Many previously disadvantaged universities have not been receiving third stream funding. South African corporate sponsors do not view supporting these institutions as part of playing their role in development; they want to have their brands associated with the prestigious universities. (Luzuko Buku, 2017)*

Funding is a pivotal issue for HEIs. Comparing the possible funding models, many universities opted to give fewer funds to more students. This tends to increase the debt burden of the universities, and funding per individual does not cover all costs. In 2009, student debt in South Africa was at R3 billion, and has been steadily increasing (HESA, 2011).

Cost of Higher Education

Over the years, government funding has not kept pace with the increase in the student population. Hence, to maintain quality whilst balancing the books, universities have had to shift the financial burden onto students. It is argued by many that attending a university in South Africa has become prohibitively expensive. For example, Fourie and Calitz (2016) showed that a BA degree at Stellenbosch University was now almost three times more expensive (in real terms) than in the 1960s.

Socio-economic, Class and Racial Inequalities

Klasen (2002) focused on gender inequality in education but arrived at similar conclusions whether considering income, gender or racial discrimination. They each result in a sub-optimal allocation of education. If education is distributed on any grounds other than merit, some capable students will not have access to higher levels of education. As it has been indicated previously, contemporary South Africa has inherited an education system, which promulgated racial and social injustices and the unequal distribution of this public good. The country still has a polarised HE system with very poor and underdeveloped institutions on the one hand and highly developed and modern institutions, on the other.

EFFORTS TOWARDS IMPROVING ACCESS TO HE IN SOUTH AFRICA

Since the end of apartheid in 1994, access to HE has been a government-stated priority. This was, and is, evidenced by initiatives such as the setting up of the National Commission on Higher Education by the Mandela government in 1995; the Green Paper on Higher Education published in 1996; the NSFAS – a statutory body under the Department of Higher Education – introduced in the late 1990s, as well as a NPHE in 2001, which pushed for equality and increased access.

Commission on Higher Education (1995)

The Commission's report proposed that South Africa establish a single, coordinated national education system that would promote increased access for the historically disadvantaged black majority (CHE, 1996). The CHE proposals revolved around three areas: participation, responsiveness and governance. Participation dealt with the problem of increasing access to HE and changing it from an elitist to a 'mass' system.

> *Bringing more poor and black students into universities and Technicons required diverse programmes, curricula and qualifications; 'multiple entry and exit points'; changes in institutional functions and structures; and more funding. A single system would address inherited inequities, inefficiencies and be able to plan and 'manage' increased access. (CHE Report, 1996, Overview)*

The CHE major recommendations informed the Green Paper on Higher Education (1996), the Draft White Paper on Higher Education (April 1997) – eventually the White Paper on Higher Education (July 1997) – and the National Plan (2001). The CHE report served as a useful introduction to the key issues, ideas and debates surrounding HE in the democratic period of South Africa's history. The Commission saw itself as producing policy that broke with a tradition of key policy texts going back to those produced under the previous regime. The universities and technicons were to be transformed so that they addressed inherited inequalities, inefficiencies faced up to new socio-economic and cultural challenges including 'the changing skill and knowledge requirements for improved productivity and innovation, and the needs associated with the building of a new citizenry' (CHE, 1996).

The National Development Plan 2030

The National Development Plan 2030 (NDP) equally addresses issues of inequality, alleviation of poverty and accessibility to HE.

The NDP's vision for 2030 is a post-school system that produces graduates who have skills to meet the current and future needs of the economy and society. The different parts of the education system should work together to allow students to take different pathways that offer high-quality learning opportunities.

According to the NDP 2030, there should be clear linkages between schools, further education and training colleges, universities of technology, and universities and other providers of education and training. There should also be clear linkages between education and training and the world of work.

National Student Financial Aid Scheme

During apartheid, the vast majority of students at HEI in South Africa were white. In 1980, for example, they constituted 74.8% of students, compared to the 12.5% that were black. A decade later in 1990, black students still represented only 37.7% of all the students (de Villiers, 1996). This disproportionate relationship between national demography and representation at tertiary institutions was a continuing reflection of the broader injustice of the previous political system.

The state has made TVET colleges and universities accessible to thousands of students in poverty through the NSFAS. The NSFAS Act was promulgated in December 1999 to give real effect to the government's commitment to redress the inequities of the past and tackle the growing student debt problem in HEIs. NSFAS and its predecessors awarded R50.5 billion to about 1.5 million students in the form of loans and bursaries between 1991 and 2014 at 25 public HEIs and 50 TVET colleges (Nxasana, 2016). The introduction of the Scheme was an initiative to counter the previous injustices and make HE more affordable for the poor, and more representative of the country's demographics.

The 'Free Education' Initiative

The #Fees-Must-Fall protest brought to light the need for a truly publicly funded HE system and it placed this demand at the door of government. In the past, the universities have hiked fees under the disguise of improving academic provision. These fee hikes are what triggered the 2015 protests. In its presentation to the Fees Commission in 2016, Statistics South Africa revealed that HE fees in South Africa increased up to 25% above inflation from 2008 to 2015 until the no-fee increase which took effect from 2016 (Commission of Enquiry, 2016)

In December 2017, President Jacob Zuma announced free HE for students from 90% of South African households. His State of the Nation Address in February 2018 and the recent Budget Speech affirmed this decision and 'free education' is being rolled out. The new funding scheme brings to the fore questions about whether this constitutes a more sustainable deal compared with existing ones, which address issues of accessibility for historically disadvantaged communities, as well as whether it is a positive step towards a more feasible and inclusive transformation agenda.

In order to tackle some of the issues raised in the NDP and as a response to the much-heated #Fees-Must-Fall protests by students in 2015 and 2016, the Zuma administration put another Commission in place (The Fees Commission). This Commission assessed the feasibility of making HE and training free. Its report acknowledges the universal right to education and the State's constitutional duty to make that right accessible and meaningful, particularly for historically disadvantaged communities. However, the financial resources remain limited. On that basis, the Commission's report proposed a cost-sharing model to fund university students. This is in the form of an income-contingent loan scheme for all students, with a provision to opt out. The state would either purchase the loans or guarantee their repayment (Commission of Enquiry, 2016).

Whilst the new 'free-education' policy is at an early stage, there are positive indications that this might present an opportunity to begin to develop a more inclusive policy, and make this 'right' meaningful to historically disadvantaged and neglected communities. However, grey areas remain in terms of how the new funding deal will be fully achieved, as well as the implications of the differential fee charges across South Africa's 21 universities of higher learning. If not closely monitored, the differences might signal new dilemmas around accessibility and inclusivity.

Public–Private Partnership Model

A process has been started to accelerate the building of a sustainable public-private partnership model. This model plans to raise enough funding to offer comprehensive financial support to students from poor and middle-income households, as well as academic, psycho-social and life-skills support. The key objective is to improve the access, success and employment of poor and 'missing middle' students as they enter, progress through, and exit HEI.

The model seeks to give effect to the constitutional requirement to improve access and opportunities for the success of students. Financial support would include a combination of grants, bursaries and loans regulated by various criteria, but with the guiding principles of reducing the financial burden on poor, means-tested households and the promotion of skills development of high-demand occupations. The loans-grants ratio will increase as the household income will increase up to a determined middle-income threshold (Prussing & Correia, 2016).

CONCLUSION

HE plays a major role in a person's life and a nation's development. This is a kind of investment and return to the individual and the nation too. The South African government, through its initiatives and efforts, recognises that HE is a 'public good' and, accordingly, must benefit from state support. Therefore, whilst fees need to be introduced, they should represent only a proportion of the actual economic cost, and should be accompanied by appropriate loan schemes or scholarships for socially and economically disadvantaged students.

South Africa has adequate resources and capacity to meet the challenges faced by the HE sector. The solutions lie in driving better co-ordination of government programmes in education generally, as well as driving better co-ordination and collaboration between the government and the private sector. South Africa has shown its resilience and ability to tackle some of its challenges. So far, policy and practice to improve access to HE in South Africa are like the Curate's Egg – good, only in parts. Greater progress will be achieved only if all stakeholders work together, driven by a common vision.

REFERENCES

Badat, S. (2010). *The challenges of transformation in higher education and training institutions in South Africa.* South Africa: Development Bank of South Africa. Retrieved from https://www.dbsa.org/EN/About-Us/Publications/Documents/ The%20challenges%20of%20transformation%20in%20 higher%20education%20and%20training%20institutions%20 in%20South%20Africa%20by%20Saleem%20Badat.pdf

Botha, D., & Takalani, T. (2008). *Barriers to e-learning amongst post graduate black students in higher education in South Africa.*

Unpublished M.Phil. dissertation, Stellenbosch University, South Africa. Retrieved from HYPERLINK "http://www/" \hhttps://www. scholar.sun.ac.za/handle/10019.1/3114

Buku, L. (2018, March 2). The equalizing effect of government's 'free education' initiative for the higher education sector. *The Daily Maverick*. Retrieved from https://www.dailymaverick.co.za/opinionista/2018-03-02-the-equalising-effect-of-governments-free-education-initiative-for-the-higher-education-sector/#.WuXFAoiFPIW

Cele, M. B. G. (2014). *Student politics and the funding of higher education in South Africa: The case of the University of the Western Cape 1995–2005*. Unpublished Ph.D. thesis, University of the Western Cape, Cape Town, South Africa. Retrieved from HYPERLINK "http://www.thepresidency.gov.za/press-state-" \hhttp://www.etd.uwc.ac.za/xmlui/handle/11394/4318

Commission of Inquiry into Higher Education. (2016). Report. Retrieved from http://www.thepresidency.gov.za/press-statements/release-report-commission-inquiry-feasibility-making-high-education-and-training

Council on Higher Education (CHE). (1996, January). NCHE Report: A Framework for Transformation. Retrieved from http://www.che.ac.za/media_and_publications/other-stakeholder-s-publications/nche-report-framework-transformation-1996

Council on Higher Education (CHE). (2016). 2013 Higher Education Data: Participation. Retrieved from http://www.che.ac.za/focus_areas/higher_education_data/2013/participation

Department of Higher Education and Training. (2017). Draft policy framework for the internationalization of higher education in South Africa. *Government Gazette, 622*, 11–23.

de Villiers, P. (1996). *The poor and access to higher education in South Africa: The NSFAS contribution*. Unpublished Ph.D. thesis, Stellenbosch University, South Africa.

de Villiers, P., Van Wyk, C., & Van Der Berg, S. (2012). The first five-year project: A cohort study of students awarded NSFAS loans in the first five years 2000-2004. Research Report for NSFAS, Brussels, European Commission. Retrieved from www.nsfas.org.za/.../Research%20Topic%20 2%20-%20A%20Cohort%20Analysis.pdf

Herschkowitz, S. (2017, April). #FeesMustFall: South African Students Fight for Higher Education. Protests against High Costs of Attendance at Higher Education Institutions Continue in South Africa. Retrieved from http://thepolitic.org/fees-mustfall-south-african-students-fight-for-higher-education

Malele, I. (2011, February 7.). Access to Higher Education: Challenges: Higher Education South Africa Briefing. Parliamentary Monitoring Group. Retrieved from https://pmg. org.za/committee-meeting/12495/

Nxasana, S. (2015, March). SA has the Means to Make Higher Education More Accessible. Retrieved from https:// issuu.com/topcomedia/docs/vision_2030_publication_2015

Pandor, N. (2015, February 12). Access to education has improved but quality poor. Interview in *Mail & Guardian* Online. Retrieved from https://mg.co.za/article/2015-02-12-access-to-education-has-improved-but-quality-poor

Prussing, T., & Correia, C. (2015). Public-private partnership in South Africa: A tale of two prisons. Paper (MAF03) pre-sented to the 2016 SAAA National Teaching and Learning and Regional Conference. Retrieved from http://www.saaa.org.za/ Downloads/2016%20SAAA%20T&L%20and%20Regional%20 Conference%20Proceedings.pdf

4

LEARNING THROUGH LIFE REVISITED: THE ROLE OF POLICY IN ENHANCING SOCIAL MOBILITY THROUGH ACCESS TO PART-TIME STUDY

Liz Marr and John Butcher

ABSTRACT

This chapter focusses on the situation of part-time learners and explores the extent to which policy in England has confounded, rather than facilitated, lifelong learning opportunities. A brief overview of Lifelong Learning policy at Pan-European level is presented with the findings of a specific project which sought to establish what the barriers were to access for diverse student bodies in England, Denmark, Finland and Germany. Then, the authors focus on the 'perfect storm'[1] in English

---

1 A 'perfect storm' is an expression sometimes used to describe a situation where an unusual combination of factors result in a severely aggravated outcome.

Higher Education where a catastrophic decline in the numbers of part-time student, generated due to the clash of several policy 'clouds', raises questions about the government's commitment to lifelong learning.

Keywords: Part-time; adult; lifelong learning; policy; economic challenges; vocational learning

INTRODUCTION

In December 2008, the European Universities Association (EUA) published a Lifelong Learning Charter (EUA, 2008), which sought to establish a shared commitment by universities and governments to what is, essentially, a widening access-and-success agenda. The impetus for production of the Charter lay not only in the social and economic challenges presented by globalisation, demographic change and technological developments, but also in the desire to foster greater inclusion and responsiveness within the higher education (HE) sector.

In its rationale, the Charter recognised that 'European societies are missing out on a huge pool of readily available human talent' (p. 4) – an assertion not so very different from that used to justify the launch of the UK Open University, almost 50 years ago (Crowther, 1969). In the context of the overall history of HE in the global north, this is a relatively short period but one in which there have been huge changes in the global HE sector, as well as major fluctuations in national ideological and policy contexts. In particular, the ideological shift to a neo-liberal, market-focussed environment has brought about a sea change in much of the HE sector (Levidow, 2002; Olssen & Peters, 2005). What this exemplifies, in relation to the themes of this book, is that widening access to HE is both driven, and challenged, by policy – a significant contributor to the conundrum of the 'curate's egg'.

Amongst the Lifelong Learning Charter commitments expected of universities, some have already been adopted, at least in principle, not only in Europe but also in the Americas and Australasia. These include:

- the embedding of widening access and lifelong learning concepts into institutional strategies;

- provision for a diverse student population;

- the adaptation of study programmes for new audiences; and

- appropriate guidance and counselling, (EUA, 2008).

However, other elements have not been quite so evenly embedded, such as:

- the recognition of prior learning;
- the consolidation of reforms for flexible and creative learning environments; and

- the development of partnerships to provide appropriate and relevant programmes of study.

These issues, nevertheless, are critical to address challenges related to skills shortages, which are exacerbated by the rapid rates of change in the demographic, technological and global contexts.

CHALLENGES TO LIFELONG LEARNING IN HIGHER EDUCATION – A EUROPEAN VIEW

The origins of European policy on lifelong learning can be found in the work of Yeaxlee (1929) and subsequent policy developments prompted by Faure et al. (1972), Delors (1996) and the Bologna Declaration of 1998 (Fearn, 2008; Hoell,

Lentsch, & Litta, 2009). Despite slow progress with the latter, reference to lifelong learning and widening partici-pation became more central to the Bologna Framework as indicated at the 2009 Leuven conference.

> *(…) Faced with the challenge of an ageing population, Europe can only succeed in this endeavour if it maximises the talents and capacities of all its citizens and **fully engages in lifelong learning as well as in widening participation in higher education**. (authors' emphasis) (Bologna, 2009)*

In their considerations, the European Higher Education Ministers emphasised that:

> *Lifelong learning implies that qualifications may be obtained through flexible learning paths, including part-time studies, as well as work-based routes*

and that

> *[s]uccessful policies for lifelong learning will include basic principles and procedures for Recognition of Prior Learning on the basis of learning outcomes regardless of whether the knowledge, skills and competencies were acquired through formal, non-formal, or informal learning paths. (Bologna, 2009)*

These ideas are now commonly appearing in European Higher Education discourses but whilst, in theory, they are recognised as critical to the maintenance of high-skill economies, there are still many barriers to their implemen-tation. The Opening Up Universities to Lifelong Learning project sought to identify some of these barriers and make recommendations for overcoming them. Based on find-ings from four countries, it was clear that in all cases the principal challenges lay within the universities themselves. Barriers caused by systems can be dismantled; however, cultures, reflecting traditional perceptions of what HE is for, are more difficult to dislodge. Thus, opening up to students from diverse backgrounds; implementing credit recognition and transfer arrangements; and facilitating transition between vocational and academic programmes of study were all resisted to varying extents, on the grounds of academic quality and standards (Muller et al., 2015).

Such resistance is still played out, despite further European Community (EC) policy directives. Most recently, the EC Directorate General for Education and Culture has announced a commitment to Short Learning Programmes: online courses of study of up to 30 ECTS,[2] which meet the needs of business and employers (Marr, 2017). Again, the delivery of this policy is highly dependent on the commitment of the HE sector as well as the will of national governments. As we will now go on to show, this is highly problematic where a country has no lifelong learning strategy or policy in place.

THE DECLINE OF PART-TIME STUDY IN ENGLAND – THE PERFECT STORM

In England, access to part-time HE, despite its critical importance to social justice, social mobility and impact on the economy (Universities UK, 2013) has been subject to catastrophic, albeit unintended, policy consequences over the last decade. Previously, the opportunity to study part-time enabled large numbers of adult learners to engage with HE. Importantly, in

---

2 ECTS – European Credit Transfer and Accumulation System is an academic credit system used throughout the European Higher Education area.

terms of widening access and lifelong learning agendas, part-time learners were disproportionately likely to be from disadvantaged backgrounds (ARC, 2013).

Around a third of undergraduates studied part-time in 2005 (HESA, 2017). Many of these students were adults in employment seeking to up-skill, or learners who had missed out at 18. They were studying later in their lives whilst juggling personal and professional responsibilities. Both groups can be perceived as students traditionally under-represented in university study. However, a sequence of HE and economic policies has eroded a previously healthy and vibrant sector, leaving part-time student numbers dramatically reduced (HEFCE, 2014, Office for Fair Access, 2017).

A perfect storm of policy commitments affecting England has contributed to this situation. These include:

- The removal of government funding for students studying for an equivalent or lower qualification (2008–2009). English universities lost funding via the direct teaching grant from the government if, as was likely for many part-timers, learners sought an employability-related qualification at an equivalent or lower level to one they had already obtained.

- A substantial reduction in employer support through training and development budgets for part-time HE study. For example, between 2010 and 2013, there was a 44% decline in students reporting employers as their main source of funding.

- Austerity policies, arising as a result of the recession, reduced public sector organisation budgets (2010–2011), impacting disproportionately on part-time student numbers in HE, as more of the public-sector workforce (up to 1.3%) studied part-time, compared to 0.7% in the economy as a whole.

- Radical changes to fee and loan arrangements (2012–2013) resulted in substantially increased tuition fees, including those for part-time study. Yet, strict eligibility criteria meant few (31%) part-time learners were eligible – often precisely those students with the characteristics which universities in England were meant to target with resources from higher fees (BIS, 2011).

- Dominant policy discourse in England around full-time HE opportunities aimed at 18-year olds drowns serious recognition of the part-time decline (Horrocks, 2017).

Within this context, part-time learners are marked by their heterogeneity (Butcher, 2015), with the widest range of personal circumstances and competing responsibilities making them a challenging group for policy makers to target. Many are the first in their families to engage with HE, and many care for family members. The impact of disability and long-term health impairments can be profound on part-time learners (Butcher & Rose-Adams, 2015)

Financial barriers have been identified as the major obstacle. In an austere economic climate, the availability of disposable income to support part-time study has diminished when housing, transport and family costs have to be prioritised. Other barriers include the lack of institutional flexibility to meet the needs of students who can only study part-time; and inadequate information, advice and guidance aimed at adults facing a bewildering complexity of part-time qualifications, entry points and financial support.

Despite this depressing outlook, there are policies that work. Even in the UK, the Celtic nations (Scotland, Wales and Northern Ireland) demonstrate a more positive and inclusive picture in terms of the numbers of part-time students. This can be explained by very different policy priorities – for example, the Welsh Assembly has made a firm commitment to part-time HE as making a vital contribution to those with protected character-istics.[3] (HEFCW, 2014). In the context of lower fee regimes, this suggests flexible and part-time study can be incentivised through the extension of living grants and loans to part-time students.

The Policy Problem

It would seem, then, that there are problems at the level of policy making as well as in its implementation. The perfect storm described previously clearly shows why getting policy right is so important. As Peter Horrocks argued (2017), it is probable that those who are making policy have limited expe-rience of the life-worlds of those whom the policy intends to support. Ministers and civil servants, in England at least, are more likely to have enjoyed the three year, full-time boarding school model of academic HE in which vocational study usu-ally refers to law or medicine, rather than construction, logis-tics or retail management. As Schuller and Watson (2009, p. 150) made clear 'one of the weaknesses of the UK system is its deep divide between academic and vocational learning, accentuated by early specialisation and narrowness of study'. They went on to argue that 'this mutual shunning has been both reflected in and reinforced by class divides'. Scott (2017) has gone further and contends that policymakers view life-long learning with 'incomprehension and condescension'.

Current policy discourse in England makes reference to social justice and social mobility, but overlooks the fact that these terms are **not** mutually interchangeable. Even had there been greater equality of opportunity in access to HE, this would not have necessarily resulted in more and better

---

3 Protected characteristics are those identified in the UK Equality Act, see
   https://www.equalityhumanrights.com/en/equality-act.

employment options in a time of austerity. There is recognition of the need to up-skill the workforce but policy itself focusses on measures to increase the number of 18-year olds entering full-time HE principally at elite institutions (see, e.g. Sundorph, Vasilev, & Coiffait, in this volume, Chapter 2). Universities themselves have embraced some concepts of lifelong learning and part-time study – in as much as they have the potential to generate income – but in the form of Continuing Professional Development short courses, rather than sustainable and accessible part-time degree routes. The closure of many Centres for Lifelong Learning by Universities across the UK suggests that without institutional commitment to expand opportunity, the prospects for adult learners in HE are at best uncertain.

One exception to this trend away from lifelong learning lies potentially in the introduction of degree apprenticeships – courses of study for trainees, paid for by employers through a levy system, which is seen as the only source of 'new' money in the sector. Alison Wolf, in her (2011) report to the English government, argued strongly for much more workplace access to strengthen the vocational offer for 14- to 19-year olds. Unhelpfully, however, apprenticeships are still commonly pitched as vocational alternatives for those somehow deemed ineligible or lacking credentials for academic study, despite such programmes requiring skills of criticality, analysis and problem solving. This raises questions about the role and purpose of HE and contributes to stratification of the HE sector where high status, research-intensive universities are regarded as the natural home for 'academic' study whilst vocational learning is concentrated in lower cost, lower status HE institutions, Further Education Colleges and Alternative Providers.

English government policy is heavily focussed on the economic returns of investment in HE for individuals and the state, and there is a considerable risk of a wider chasm emerging between 'education' for one section of society and 'training' for the rest. Apart from the moral and ethical issues this raises, the development of higher-level practical skills without the ability to critically reflect or make autonomous decisions about their deployment can severely limit their effectiveness and potential to enhance economic performance. However, there is a deeper dilemma here – selling the benefits of HE on the basis of future income potential masks the considerable differences in the distribution of such benefits, especially in the context of austerity measures.

What Does this Mean and What Can be Done?

The perfect storm of English policy and the move away from the influence of a united EC signal little hope for a renewed emphasis on lifelong learning in England. We argue here that the only way in which working populations can be sufficiently up skilled to meet immediate global economic challenges is by ensuring that there is a focus on opportunities for adults, as well as 18 years old, and that part-time study is accorded the same support, financially and politically, as full time.

There are, then, clear indicators of a need for a genuine lifelong learning policy – in England at least – but also more widely. The rapid rise in use of technology in the workplace, the growth of portfolio careers,[4] or the gig economy,[5] and the need for frequent retraining over a longer working life, all throw into question the current model of HE. Despite the obvious need for a more flexible model which recognises the

---

4 A 'portfolio career' is one in which a traditional full-time job is replaced by multiple part-time, self-employed and consultancy roles.

5 A 'gig economy' refers to a labour market, which is characterised by short-term contracts or freelance work, as opposed to permanent employment.

needs of future economies and of adults already in the work-place, policy-makers persist in reproducing models which fetishise the 'good degree' as the only currency in the career market place. Certificates, diplomas and even modular study are seen as somehow unworthy of recognition, even though they may be all that is needed at a particular point in the learner's life journey.

Advances in technology have helped, particularly with the growth of online provision and the near ubiquity of mobile devices. Massive Open Online Courses (MOOCs) promised considerable disruption (Yuan & Powell, 2013). However, the market for MOOCs is largely a professional one with most users already holding higher-level qualifications and the necessary accompanying accreditation and recognition schemes being slower to evolve (Marr, 2017; Talbot, 2017). Information, advice and guidance for adults and part-time learners are clearly needed, but currently take second place to that provided for school leavers.

CONCLUSION

So what of the curate's egg and policy for widening access and lifelong learning? MOOCs may not quite be the answer, but there is a myriad of opportunities for institutions to demonstrate a genuine commitment to learning through life. Institutional responses to a market approach need not lim-it provision to specific age cohorts or modes of study, and innovation in delivery models or course design need not com-promise standards. Indeed, one might argue these are logical responses to an increasingly competitive HE environment. At the same time, they are inclusive and focus on the needs of students. In a context where part-time can be seen as a proxy for adult learners, this is crucial.

The conundrum here is that universities have arguably never been more relevant than at a time when there are no longer 'jobs for life'. The need to retrain, update skills or change career direction will be essential as technologies and markets change and develop more and more frequently. Adults already in work, or displaced from defunct sectors, will need to study flexibly and in new and different ways. This will require new models of delivery, wider recognition of what counts as academic credential and funding schemes, which incentivise rather than deter participation. There remains, however, a serious disconnect between these require-ments and policies which persist in focussing on 18-year-olds studying full-time and segmenting them at an early age into either academic or vocational futures. The infatuation with full-time, academic HE study as the gold standard appears to be a peculiarly English disease and one which policy makers must address as a matter of urgency.

REFERENCES

ARC Network. (2013). Literature Review of Research into Widening Participation to Higher Education. Retrieved from http://offa.org.uk/wp-contents-uploads/2013/08/Literature-review-of-research-into-WP-to-HE.pdf

BIS. (2011, July). Students at the heart of the system. *TSO*. Retrieved from https://www.gov.uk/government/uploads/system/uploads/attachment_data/file/31384/11-944-higher-education-students-at-heart-of-system.pdf

Bologna, L. (2009). The Bologna Process 2020 – The European Higher Education Area in the New Decade. Retrieved from http://media.ehea.info/file/2009_Leuven_Louvain-la-Neuve/06/1/

Leuven_Louvain-la-Neuve_Communique_
April_2009_595061.pdf

Butcher, J. (2015). 'Shoe-horned and side-lined'? Challenges
for part-time learners in the new HE landscape. York:
Higher Education Academy. Retrieved from https://www.
heacademy.ac.uk/resource/shoe-horned-and-side-lined-chal-
lenges-part-time-learners-new-he-landscape

Butcher, J., & Rose-Adams, J. (2015). Part-time learners in open and distance learning: Revisiting the critical
importance of choice, flexibility and employability. Open
Learning: The Journal of Open, Distance and e-Learning,
30(2), 127–137. doi: org/10.1080/02680513.2015.1055719

Crowther, G. (1969). Speech by Lord Crowther, First
Chancellor of The Open University at the Presentation of
the Charter [Transcript]. Retrieved from https://www.open.
ac.uk/library/digital-archive/pdf/script/script:5747089b4a53f

Delors, J. (1996). Learning: The treasure within: Report to
UNESCO of the International Commission on Education
for the twenty-first century. Paris: UNESCO Publishing.

EUA. (2008). Lifelong Learning Charter. Retrieved from
http://www.eua.be/Libraries/higher-education/eua_charter_
eng_ly-(5).pdf?sfvrsn=0

Faure, E., Herrera, F., Kaddoura, A., Lopes, H., Petrovsky, A.
V., Rahnema, M., & Ward, F. C. (1972). Learning to be: The
world of education today and tomorrow. Paris: UNESCO
Publishing.

Fearn, H. (2008). The long and the short of it. Times Higher
Education, October 2–8.

HEFCE. (2014). Pressure from All Sides: Economic
and Policy Influences on Part-Time Higher Education.
Retrieved from http://www.hefce.ac.uk/media/hefce/content/
pubs/2014/201408d/HEFE2014_08d.pdf

HEFCW. (2014). Part-Time Higher Education: Position
Statement. Retrieved from http://www.hefcw.ac.uk/
documents/publications/circulars/circulars_2014W14%20
24HE%20HEFCW%20Part-time%20Higher%20
Education%20Position%20Statement.pdf

HESA. (2017). Higher Education Student Enrolments
and Qualifications Obtained at Higher Education
Providers in the United Kingdom 2015/16. Retrieved
from https://www.hesa.ac.uk/news/12-01-2017/
sfr242-students-enrolments-and-qualifications

Hoell, R., Lentsch, J., & Litta, S. (2009). The Bologna
Process: A Weary Leap Forward. *International Higher
Education*, 55(*Spring*), 9–10.

Horrocks, P. (2017, October 17). The real casualty of the
2012 tuition fees shake-up? Mature and part-time learners.
UUK blog. Retrieved from http://www.universitiesuk.ac.uk/
blog/Pages/The-real-casualty-of-2012-tuition-fees-shake-up-
mature-and-part-time-learners.aspx

Levidow, L. (2002). Marketizing higher education:
Neoliberal strategies and counter-strategies. In K. Robins
& F. Webster (Eds.), *The Virtual University? Knowledge,
markets and management* (pp. 227–248). Oxford: Oxford
University Press.

Marr, L. (2017, January). *Learning without boundaries:
Short Learning Programmes and international collaboration*. Keynote speech at internationalisation in a digital age
Maastricht Innovation in Higher Education Days (MID
2017), Maastricht.

Muller, R., Remdisch, S., Kohler, K., Marr, L., Repo, S., &
Ynigegn, C. (2015). Easing access for lifelong learners: A com-
parison of European models for university lifelong learning.
International Journal of Lifelong Education, 34(5) 530–550.

Office for Fair Access. (2017). *Strategic guidance: Developing your 2018/19 access agreement*. Retrieved from https://www.OFFA.org.uk/wp-content/uploads/2017/02/ Strategic-guidance-devloping-your-2018-19-access-agreement-FINAL.pdf.

Olssen, M., & Peters, A. (2005). Neoliberalism, higher education and the knowledge economy: From the free market to knowledge capitalism. *Journal of Education Policy*, *20*(3), 313–345.

Schuller, T., & Watson, D. (2009). *Learning through life: Inquiry into the future of lifelong learning*. Leicester: NIACE.

Scott, P. (2017, May 25). Fair access, lifelong learning and social justice. Keynote address at the *Widening Access Seminar: The Place of Adult Learning in Widening Access to Higher Education: Exploring Current Policy and Practice in Scotland*, The Open University, Glasgow.

Talbot, J. (2017). Repurposing MOOCs for the accreditation of prior learning: A survey of practice in university work based learning departments. *Widening Participation and Lifelong Learning*, *199*(3), 113–136.

Universities UK. (2013). The Power of Part-Time: Review of Part-Time and Mature Higher Education. Retrieved from http://www.universitiesuk.ac.uk/highereducation/ Documents/2013/PowerOfPartTime.pdf

Wolf, A. (2011). *Review of vocational education*. London: Department for Education.

Yeaxlee, B. (1929). *Lifelong education*. London: Cassell.

Yuan, L., & Powell, S. (2013). MOOCs and open education: Implications for higher education. CETIS/JISC. Retrieved from http://publications.cetis.ac.uk/2013/667

5

INCREASING ACCESS TO TERTIARY AND HIGHER EDUCATION IN RURAL COMMUNITIES: EXPERIENCES FROM TASMANIA AND NEW ZEALAND

Margaret Noble and Jessica Grant

ABSTRACT

Access to higher education (HE) in rural and coastal communities has been a developing area of research over the last two decades. This chapter looks at the particular issues of access and participation facing tertiary institutions in the context of Tasmania (Australia) and New Zealand. Both locations in the southern hemisphere have particular cultural, social and geographical circumstances and are characterised by dispersed rural and regional communities over extensive geographical areas and considerable tracts of remote territory. They share strong similarities to the issues facing access and inclusion in HE in the northern hemisphere and globally.

Keywords: Access; participation; rural; tertiary; Tasmania; New Zealand; partnership

INTRODUCTION

A wide body of research shows that a number of common factors affect access to, and participation in, higher education (HE) in rural communities (Behrendt, 2012; Bridge Group, 2017; Kilpatrick, 2004; Shah, 2016; Welch, 2007). There is an overwhelming view that geography combines with socio-economic and historical factors in rural areas to compound disadvantage and adversely impact on the propensity to participate in HE (Halsey, 2017; NCSEHE, 2017; Webb, 2015; Woodroffe & Kilpatrick, 2017). Complex intersections of people and places and a range of structural and cultural factors, primarily determined by place, combine to inform student choices and outcomes about future study options. Place can be a limiting factor for many potential students who identify strongly with their local region and are often discouraged from choosing education pathways different to those of their family or which mean leaving their home community (Halsey, 2017; Woodroffe & Kilpatrick, 2017).

Many rural and regional areas are also adversely impacted by the increasing economic and cultural dominance of major urban centres (Bridge Group, 2017). Whilst much has been written about barriers to access and participation in rural, remote and coastal regions, it is evident that many of the barriers to access and participation are similar to those faced by lower socio-economic background students in urban areas. The main difference is that barriers tend to be more pronounced in rural areas due to generally lower levels of income, poor transport connectivity, and often lower social aspirations and expectations amongst residents.

GENERAL ISSUES FOR TERTIARY AND HE INSTITUTIONS

There is an increasing body of research about the strategies that have been, and should be, adopted to increase participation. Interventions that have been trialled include: aspiration-raising activities; pathway and transition initiatives with schools; provision of locally available foundation, access and enabling programmes; the establishment of local/community learning hubs and new HE centres and work with communities (Action on Access, 2005; Crawford, 2014; Gaskell, 2017; NCESHE, 2017; see also Gaskell & Dunn in this volume, Chapter 12). These initiatives are designed to make young people aware that HE is a possible trajectory, through provision of information and activities to help and support them to develop appropriate pathways.

When institutions seek to increase participation rates in HE by those from rural communities, they face issues in both changing what are often long-established cultural patterns of limited participation, and in delivering accessible provision. It requires institutions to respond in a number of areas viz.:

- delivering a social/community mission - being cognisant of the different cultural perceptions and perspectives of communities;

- stakeholder engagement - establishing strong partnerships with schools, communities and government; and

- resourcing distributed provision - ensuring adequate resourcing across multiple delivery locations; addressing issues of providing a comparable high-quality learning experience and strong support services and determining the depth and breadth of the curriculum offer.

TASMANIA

Tasmania has a very distinctive position in the Australian HE landscape. It has historic low levels of participation in HE that consistently sit well below the national average. Tasmanians have been described by Susan Parr, Chair of the Tasmanian Chamber of Commerce and Industry, as 'the unhealthiest, oldest, worst educated, most under-employed and most dependent on government benefits in Australia' (Eslake, 2016, p. 1). Within the State, there has been a longstanding divide in education attainment between the major urban area represented by the capital, Hobart, and regional Tasmania with the North West of the region particularly experiencing poor educational outcomes.

Considerable research has been undertaken to look at the issues facing educational attainment in Tasmania. Eslake (2016) has argued that

> *The single most important thing that needs*
> *to be done in order to improve Tasmanian's*
> *material living standards relative to those of other*
> *Australians is to increase the levels of educational*
> *participation and attainment, which despites some*
> *improvements in recent years, remains significantly*
> *behind most other parts of Australia. (p. 91)*

Australian Bureau of Statistics (ABS) data show that only about 19.3% of the population aged 15–75 years has a bachelor's degree or higher qualification compared to a national average of over 26% (ABS, 2017). Nearly one in five of the population (19.4%) aged 15–75 years left school in year 10 and has no further qualifications compared to a national average of 11.5% (ABS, 2016). Within the North West of the region, participation in HE is circa 8% and in the North in the Launceston region, it is 13%, which is in sharp contrast with a participation rate of over 20% in the South, around the capital Hobart. These figures are below overall levels of HE participation in Australia and significantly lower than those in other OECD countries.

The UK, for example, set a target in 1999 to achieve 50% participation by young people in HE and recent evidence shows that current levels sit at 49% (Grove, 2017; UK Department for Education, 2017). Tasmanian patterns of participation in HE have been impacted by:

- a low density and dispersed regional population;

- a region suffering from poor social mobility;

- relative geographic isolation; and

- a culture in which leaving school at year 10 has been the norm (Eslake, 2016).

As the only university in the State, the University of Tasmania plays a key role in increasing access to HE. It is addressing this through a number of strategies to:

- create a distinctive education system to support access;

- establish strong partnerships;

- adopt innovative curriculum design;

- introduce a transformation program to increase regional access; and

- increase the range of outreach activities.

Established in 1890, the University hosts approximately 37,000 students including 8,000 international students
(Rathjen, 2017). The University took a strategic decision to
ensure that it is centrally involved in improving educational
attainment and access to education in Tasmania and adopted
a model to create 'an integrated university system' (Rathjen,
2017). The model is based on a state-wide approach to deliver HE regionally 'where the need for increased university participation is greatest and the advantages of community-based
access are most acute' (Rathjen, 2017, p. 3).

Partnerships

It is recognised that changing long-held patterns of education in
Tasmania, whereby traditionally many young people left school
at the end of grade 10 and there is an undervaluing of the potential advantages of HE pathways by many communities, can only
be changed through strong partnership working. Central to the
University of Tasmania model is the partnership with the State
Government; *'Making the Future Partnership'* (UTAS, 2015)
articulates the shared commitment and objectives of improving the economic and social future of Tasmania. Partnership
initiatives with the State include City Deal in Launceston and
establishment of The Peter Underwood Centre for Educational
Attainment. Of equal importance are relationships across local
government, schools, local communities and industry. A priority
has also been to develop a partnership with TasTAFE,[1] as principal provider of further and vocational education, through investigating both pathway articulation between tertiary programmes
and the development of shared infrastructure and services.

---

1 **TasTAFE** is a Tasmanian tertiary education body of the Australian state-
based Technical and Further Education system run by the Tasmanian State
Government.

Regional Access

A transformative plan is underway to offer learning across Tasmania's regions through both state-wide degrees, and revitalisation of regional campuses which are an integral part of close-knit rural and regional communities. This is akin to initiatives seen in other countries and regions such as Scarborough in the UK (Gaskell, 2017; Gaskell & Dunn in this volume, Chapter 12). Ambitious infrastructure programmes have commenced in Burnie (population circa 20,000) in the North West, Launceston (population circa 81,000) in the North, and Hobart (population circa 220,000) in the South. The aim is to bring HE into the hearts of these communities and improve the visibility, learning access and cultural connection with the University.

Outreach activities focus on three distinct phases for young people of: informing aspirations, building pathways and transition programmes. Initiatives to inform early aspiration include the 'Children's University Tasmania[2]', offering children aged 7–14 years educational experiences outside of school and recognising their achievements through the award of formal certificates and graduations. For pathways, the partnership with the Department of Education's *My Education* team and TasTAFE through *Creating My Career*, for example, enables young people to explore career and study pathways across 19 subject areas. Transition initiatives include both the University Connections Program, enabling senior secondary students to complement their curriculum with university level study, and foundation and pathway programmes.

---

2 Children's University Australia is an international partner of Children's University Trust (UK) and managed by the University of Adelaide, South Australia.

Curriculum Design

Curriculum change has been central in meeting educational needs in Tasmania. Three key issues were identified as necessary to increase participation – affordability, regional delivery and relevance (Rathjen, 2017). Applied vocational two-year Associate Degrees have been developed and are offered through the institution's University College with flexible delivery and progression pathways connected to the needs of industry, communities and the economy. The broader undergraduate curriculum has been redesigned so that it:

- responds more effectively to students' needs;

- provides different entry points into HE;

- is accessible across the whole State;

- incorporates work-integrated learning; and

- builds on research excellence.

NEW ZEALAND

With a land mass 10% bigger than the UK, but with a population of 4.7 million heavily concentrated in major urban centres of Auckland, Wellington, Hamilton, Christchurch and Dunedin, the challenge of serving dispersed regional communities in New Zealand is considerable. Offering HE provision outside of the major urban centres is challenging, particularly in achieving viable student numbers where transport connectivity and digital access are often poor.

In rural areas, participation rates in tertiary education remain low, especially amongst the Māori and Pasifika populations. In 2015, 9.8% of the population aged 15 years and over participated in tertiary education, compared to 10.2% in 2014 and 12% in 2010 (Education Counts, 2017)[3]. Over the period 2008–2016, there has been a decline of 75,000 students participating in tertiary enrolments at pre degree level compensated for by some growth in degree and postgraduate enrolments (Education Counts, 2017).

Important factors affecting HE participation are the achievement levels in secondary education and disparity between rates of attainment and transition to tertiary education by particular ethnic groups. The disparity between achievement of the National Certificate in Educational Achievement (NCEA level 2 and NCEA level 3 which provides the benchmark for university entrance[4]), is marked. In 2016 at NCEA level 2, 66% of Māori achieved the qualification compared to a NZ average for all students of over 80%, and just 34% of Māori achieved NCEA level 3 compared to 54% of all students.

Bay of Plenty Region

With just over 300,000 inhabitants, the Bay of Plenty Region in the central North Island provides some examples of the institutional and regional strategies to increase access and participation. The region is one of contrasts: the western area and the port of Tauranga experiences population growth and economic expansion; the central and Eastern areas are characterised by dispersed rural populations, economic stability or decline and high concentrations of Māori, in particular a growing proportion of Māori youth. More than 66% of schools exhibit high scores on indices of multiple deprivation. Levels of achievement and qualification at both school

---

3 NZ Ministry of Education website providing information about education statistics and research.

4 GCSE and A-level equivalent

leaving age and at tertiary level, although increasing, are generally below the national average. In particular, there are significant achievement and tertiary progression gaps between Māori students and those of all other learners.

The region has been historically served by two Institutes of Technology – Bay of Plenty Polytechnic and Waiariki Institute of Technology – and one regional *wānanga*,[5] together with some provision by the University of Waikato and a number of private tertiary education establishments. In 2016, the two institutes merged to form a new larger institution for the region, Toi Ohomai Institute of Technology. This merger was a response to the need to increase scale, avoid overlapping competition and hence diverting of demand, and more importantly to reach out to the dispersed rural community (BoPP, 2015).

One of the challenges facing the region's institutions working to support increased tertiary access has been limited equity funding and the absence of additional funding for regional and remote provision. Institutions have thus had to adopt a range of strategic responses to ensure that the region's skills needs are met and the needs of individuals and communities can be addressed.

Education Partnerships

A tertiary partnership for the region was established in 2013 between four institutions – University of Waikato, Awanuiarangi, Bay of Plenty Polytechnic and Waiariki Institute of Technology. The institutions agreed to work collaboratively to avoid competition and duplication of provision, increase tertiary pathways and to develop programmes aligned to the region's needs, thereby unlocking regional potential and latent demand. In partnership with the region's Economic Develop-

---

5 In the education system of New Zealand, a *wānanga* is a publicly owned
   tertiary institution that provides education in a Māori cultural context.

ment Association, a *Tertiary Intentions Strategy for Bay of Plenty* region was developed with the aim of encouraging and supporting engagement in tertiary education and a commitment to regional provision and locally available learning (Bay of Connections, 2014). Members of the partnership also worked together to open up new study locations including the development of the Tauranga Tertiary campus as well as participating collaboratively in government initiatives. Waiariki Institute of Technology and the Bay of Plenty Polytechnic jointly participated in the Trades Academy, a programme whereby school students could study vocational tertiary education and gain both vocational and academic qualifications, and in the Secondary Tertiary Alignment Resource enabling students to gain a taste of tertiary subjects whilst at school.

Institutional Initiatives

Individual institutions also took strategic decisions to open up access as the example of Waiariki Institute of Technology (now Toi OhoMai Institute of Technology) shows. Waiariki had a long commitment to regional provision offering courses through a network of campuses (Fig. 1). The institution's strategy was to locate provision at all levels – Level 2 (foundation) to level 9 (postgraduate) – at the main Rotorua campus, but to locate provision up to level 5 at regional campuses in Whakatane, Taupo and Tokoroa, the latter campus a joint tertiary learning centre with the national wānanga – Te Wānanga o Aotearoa.

This regional provision strategy was supported through an inter-campus bus network to ensure that students who commenced certificate level study could progress through to diploma qualifications and beyond. Whilst this was a significant cost to the institution, it was greatly valued by the community and served to encourage progression to higher levels of learning.

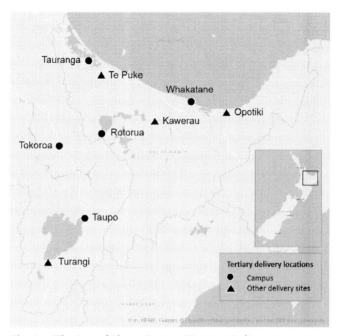

Fig. 1. The Bay of Plenty Region: Tertiary Delivery Locations.

A commitment was also made to offer courses, primarily at levels 2 and 3, at other delivery locations where strong partnerships were established with iwi and hapu communities and Trusts; for example, the delivery of a programme in Health, Disability and Aged Support at Kawerau, and courses in farming and forestry in Turangi. To create synergy with iwi educational plans much local provision was located on maraes (sacred meeting grounds which are the focal point of Māori communities) and used local tutors from Māori communities with whom students could identify.

It is difficult to measure the direct impact of some of these initiatives due to lead in times and the complex learning pathways taken by many students from low socio-economic backgrounds. However, within the region, there is an evidence of increasing attainment rates in schools and increased transition to tertiary education particularly amongst the Māori community.

CONCLUSION

The need to increase access to tertiary and higher education in rural areas in both New Zealand and Tasmania has identified a number of practices that could be adopted to support increased participation in tertiary education in other rural areas. These include the importance of:

- understanding the geography, culture and landscape that affect access and participation;

- reaching out to new communities and locations – drawing on the available resources of those communities and taking time to understand partner and community aspirations;

- creating new learning pathways and building progression routes for students, especially in local communities whilst ensuring that provision is flexible;

- offering subjects/programmes relevant to regional and community needs, and which are culturally relevant;

- creating complementarity in provision between different providers;

- increasing the availability of local provision and delivering at welcoming study sites;

- demystifying provision and making students aware of the range of entry and study options; and

- establishing close partnerships with external stakeholders – government, schools, communities, business and other tertiary providers.

Overall, it is important that there are regionally relevant responses. This necessitates working through partnerships to build regional and community confidence and draw on community bonding to build capacity in communities. Cultural change takes time and tertiary and HE institutions have to be aware that they are investing in long-term strategies, which can become embedded within communities and are not just about quick returns.

REFERENCES

Action on Access. (2005). A Rough Guide for Higher Education Providers. Retrieved from https://www.heacademy.ac.uk/system/files/widening_participation_roughguide_for_education_providers.pdf https://www.heacademy.ac.uk/workstreams-research/themes/...access.../action-access

Bay of Connections. (2014). Bay of Plenty Tertiary Intentions Strategy 2014–2019: A Regional Plan for the Strategic Alignment and Development of Post-Secondary Education and Research. Retrieved from http://www.bayofconnections.com/downloads/TIS-%20summary_final_web.pdf

Bay of Plenty Polytechnic, Waiariki Institute of Technology. 2015. Increasing Collaboration between the Bay of Plenty Polytechnic and Waiariki Institute of Technology: Single Stage Business Case. Retrieved from https://dow.tec.govt.nz/Documents/Publications/BoPP-Waiariki-Business-Case.pdf

Behrendt, l., Larkin, S., Griew, R., & Kelly, P . (2012). *Review of higher education access and outcomes for Aboriginal and Torres Strait islander people*. Final report. Canberra: Australian Government.

Bridge Group. (2017, May). *Rural and disadvantage working group, the importance of place: Progression to higher education in rural and coastal communities*. Update Briefing. London: The Bridge Group.

Crawford. N. (2014). Practical and profound: Multilayered benefits of a university enabling program and implications for higher education. *International Studies in Widening Participation*, *1*(2), 15–30.

Education Counts. (2017). Retrieved from https://www.educationcounts.govt.nz/statistics/tertiary-education/participation

Eslake, S. (2016). *Tasmania report 2016*. Tasmania: Tasmanian Chamber of Commerce and Industry.

Gaskell, C. (2017, December). Leading small scale, new and evolving higher education institutions in turbulent times. SRHE International Conference, Wales.

Grove, J. (2017, December 7). How can widening participation best be achieved?. *Times Higher Education Supplement (THE)*. retrieved from https://www.timeshighereducation.com/features/how-can-widening-participation-best-be-achieved

Halsey, J. (2017). *Independent review into regional, rural and remote education discussion paper*. Australia: Commonwealth of Australia.

Kilpatrick, S., & Loechel, B. (2004). Interactional infrastructure in rural communities: Matching training needs and provision. *Rural Society*, *14*(1), 4–21.

NCSEHE. (2017). NCSEHE Focus: Successful Outcomes for Regional and Remote Students in Australian Higher Education. Retrieved from https://www.ncsehe.edu.au/publications

Rathjen, P. (2017, October). Reflections on higher education in the Tasmanian context: The role of the University of

Tasmania in positioning education at the heart of Tasmania's future – The place of a state-wide university system in revitalising Tasmanian communities. Occasional paper University of Tasmania, Tasmania.

Shah, M., Bennett, A., & Southgate, E. (2016). *Widening higher education participation: A global perspective.* Australia: Elsevier.

UK Department for Education. (2017, September 28). Participation Rates in Higher Education: Academic Years 2006/2007–2015/2016, SFR47/2017. Retrieved from https:// www.gov.uk/government/uploads/system/uploads/attachment_ data/file/648165/HEIPR_PUBLICATION_2015-16.pdf.

UTAS. (2015). Retrieved from http://www.utas.edu. au/data/assets/pdf_file/0009/855324/State-and-UTAS-Partnership-2015.pdf

Webb, S., Black, R., Morton, R., Plowright, S., & Roy, R. (2015). *Geographical and place dimensions of post school participation in education and work.* Research report. Adelaide: Australia.

Welch, A., Helme, S., & Lamb, S. (2007). Rurality and ine-quality in education: The Australian experience. In R. Teese, S. Lamb, & M. Duru-Bellat (Eds.), *International studies in educational inequality, theory and policy* (pp. 602–604). The Netherlands: Springer

Woodroffe, J., Kilpatrick, S., Williams, B., & Jago, M. (2017). Preparing rural and regional students for the future world of work: Developing authentic career focussed curriculum through a collaborative partnership model. *Australian and International Journal of Rural Education,* 27(3), 158–173.

SECTION B

FOCUSSING ON STUDENT SUCCESS AND SOCIAL MOBILITY

6

WHAT CAN SOCIAL CAPITAL CONTRIBUTE TO STUDENT SUCCESS IN HIGHER EDUCATION? PERSPECTIVES FROM STUDENTS AND INSTITUTIONS

Helen May and Mark Jones

ABSTRACT

In recent years, there have been a growing number of references to social capital, in debates about higher education (HE), by policy makers, senior institutional leaders and academics. This chapter highlights the value of social capital to both students and institutions alike, as a contributing factor to the transformational effect of HE; and as an important tool to explain the value of HE to policy makers and the public. We draw on empirical data from students articulating the value of social capital. Their voices demonstrate that social capital has a significant role to play in institutional endeavours to maximise student success.

Keywords: Social capital; student success; higher education; social value; transformation; employability

WHAT IS SOCIAL CAPITAL?

Social capital has been raised as a matter for consideration in the context of a number of current higher education (HE) priorities such as eliminating discrimination and inequality; promoting student engagement, autonomy and responsibility; embedding employability and retention; supporting personal development and enabling student mobility. Given its prevalence, one could be forgiven for believing social capital is a panacea and yet its value to individuals, institutions and to the sector has not been clearly articulated. Efforts to demonstrate its value have centred on economic rather than social criteria, and the concept remains a contested one.

Whilst there is a vast body of literature on the topic, much of it draws upon the seminal work of Bourdieu (1986, 1996). He situates social capital alongside other forms of capital, particularly cultural and economic capital, and argues that social capital represents 'the aggregate of the actual or potential resources which are linked to possession of a durable network, or in other words membership of a group' (1986). His definition of social capital focusses on the collectively owned capital (Naidoo, 2015); hence, the capital held within and by a community that members can access.

Across the various definitions of social capital, a key point of contention is the extent to which social capital is something that is held internally and determines how an individual relates to, and learns from, others, versus something collective that is held external to an individual by a group or community. This distinction is discussed further in other contexts (Claridge, 2004) and is outside the scope of this chapter. The premise for this chapter is that social capital can be held both internally and externally.

Individual HE students will have contacts, relationships and networks they can draw on, as well as the capacity to create, conduct and apply the learning from these interactions over time. An individual's social capital could thus be enhanced within a HE context through the various relationships, networks and engagements that are available for them to capitalise on.

In research conducted for the Higher Education Academy (HEA, now Advance HE), students within two Higher Education Institutions (HEIs) were asked to define the biggest benefit of social capital[1]. Their responses were entered into a word cloud (Fig. 1). From this, it is possible to distinguish what social capital means to them.

With the most frequently occurring words appearing larger, and excluding the obvious focus on 'social' and 'capital', the three most common words are 'people', 'career' and 'able'. These words indicate the value they place on interaction, what it enables them to achieve and with a focus on the future.

THE IMPLICATIONS OF SOCIAL CAPITAL FOR STUDENT SUCCESS

The social capital literature draws attention to many and varied benefits of participating in social groups,[2] yet **access** to such groups would first be essential. This raises many ques-

---

1 Over 75 students participated in this research. Many of the students who participated were self-selecting, responding to an open call. In one institution, a cohort of students studying an enterprise module was involved. There was a mix of male and female students, at different stages of their studies and studying a range of subject areas.

2 Unless otherwise stated, social groups are used throughout this chapter as a shorthand to include networks, communities, peers, clubs/societies, initiatives and opportunities.

Fig. 1. Word Cloud of Students' Perceptions of the
Benefits of Social Capital.

tions about who gains access to what. The UK HE system,
like many across the world, dictates particular conditions
to entitle students access to what it offers – whether this is
through qualifications, awards or wider experiences. Selection
processes are predicated upon individuals being able to differentiate themselves from others. Competition affects access
into HE, into certain opportunities within HE (such as internships, mobility opportunities and elected positions), as well as
after HE into employment, further study, or apprenticeships.

To access education and the opportunities within it, an
applicant needs to stand out – not just on the basis of academic
achievements, but also on evidence drawn from group participation. Thus, the access individuals have been granted to social
groups previously can provide certain advantages that increase
the chances of future access into particular study contexts, courses, jobs, finances, resources or opportunities. Therefore, the social
capital debate is closely aligned with that about social mobility
through access to HE (see also Sundorph, Vasilev, & Coiffait on
'contextualised admissions' in this volume, Chapter 2).

The second feature of the literature on social capital is **awareness.** To gain access to social groups, it is necessary for an individual to have a degree of awareness of the existence of them, as well as an awareness of what they may gain from engaging with others in these arenas. These may be brought to a student's awareness through school, the internet, local community, national schemes or initiatives, family and friends or social media amongst others.

Having access to these arenas and opportunities does not necessarily result in individuals deriving benefits from them, intended or otherwise. Investing time in raising student awareness of the benefits of participation in social groups may well bolster their decision to engage as well as enhance the value they may derive from doing so.

The third issue is one of **trust.** Within the social capital literature (for example Coleman, 1988 and Putnam, 2000) trust is regarded as fundamental. Putnam (2000, p. 19), for example, defines social capital as referring:

> ... *to connections among individuals – social networks and the norms of reciprocity and trustworthiness that arise from them*

Whilst authors like Putnam refer to a sense of collective trust ('norms') held within a social group or network, it can also follow that individuals would need an element of trust to want to engage in, or derive benefit from, any social context.

STUDENTS' PERCEPTIONS OF THE BENEFIT OF SOCIAL CAPITAL

In 2016, as part of work commissioned by the HEA on social capital, research was conducted within two institutions by

Business Lab[3]. This was undertaken to understand how students' social capital could be effectively developed, measured and evaluated over time. As part of the work, all students were asked to complete the following sentence:

The biggest benefit of social capital is...

The analysis of these data – specifically for the purpose of this chapter – showed that social capital could be associated with the enhancement of four inter-connected areas of student success.

CONNECTIONS AND RELATIONS

The first emergent category amongst responses related to the benefit derived from building connections and relations with people. Some students simply stated the biggest benefit to be establishing friendships or relationships, whether socially or academically. Others focussed on the benefit of contact with a range of people. For example,

Social capital is particularly beneficial for us to be able to interact with different people from different culture and countries.

Having contacts which will enable you to call in favours in the future. The idea of it's who you know not what you know.

Students referred to social capital being of mutual benefit to themselves and others; about being able to give as well as receive. They spoke of receiving support, motivation and

---

3 BusinessLab is a UK-based strategy consultancy (http://www.businesslab.co.uk).

information from others, in addition to being able to share knowledge and ideas with each other and/or enrich the lives of those around them. For example,

> *It's possible to put others in contact with the right people as well as finding the right people in order to achieve the best outcome.*

> *Social capital enables we, as human beings, to trust and help each other in life.*

Amongst those referring to connections and relations, there were multiple references to networks. One student stated:

> *I believe that the social capital I have built up whilst at university enriches my life and the networks I am involved in have given and will give me opportunities that I may not have known about otherwise.*

For some students, the quality of those networks was paramount. One student spoke of having 'strongly connected networks' being the factor that 'opens opportunities'. In some regards, this was about access to opportunities but others defined access to friendship, the skills and expertise of others, or of different perspectives or approaches.

EMPLOYABILITY

Employability featured prominently amongst student responses in terms of it contributing to fulfilment of personal objectives, goals or career aspirations. This is exemplified below:

> *The biggest benefit of social capital is for me that it can offer you opportunities around the globe should you get stuck on your career path.*

> *Being able to communicate with like-minded people*
> *who could potentially help you to further your*
> *career.*

For one student, social capital was regarded as something that would enable them to be more flexible in their career:

> *If you ever wanted to change career, get in contact*
> *with someone from a certain business area, learn*
> *about other areas then it would be easy.*

Another saw social capital as important for their discipline, recognising that 'It is very difficult in my career path (music) to proceed if you are not well connected'.

PERSONAL DEVELOPMENT

There was a strong sense that social capital could contribute to personal development. Students spoke directly of the benefits they had derived from social capital, in terms of their confidence, the knowledge, insights or skills they had gained, or resources they had access to through others.

One student referred to the biggest benefit as 'building self-confidence, empathy and self-acceptance'. Another student stated that it helped 'open my eyes and receive more new ideas to motivate my mind'. Another stated that the biggest benefit was:

> *Providing an individual with the necessary social*
> *means to progress throughout life in the most*
> *effective manner.*

Within this statement, the method or process by which one can succeed is valued, as can be acquired through personal development.

QUALITY AND EFFICIENCY

Underpinning a number of responses was the notion of an efficiency or quality-gain derived from social capital: it acted as an enabler. Improvements in quality or efficiency emerged amongst a number of responses; yet, not mutually exclusive of other categories. In this regard, students referred to social capital as making things more efficient and effective; or easier for them; or even helping them to be more professional. One student focussed on social capital as an enabling factor by specifying that its biggest benefit is:

> *Being able to be as efficient as possible, utilising every resource at hand without having to create all those skills yourself. Being able to outsource tasks.*

STUDENT SUCCESS

Amongst student responses was both a personal and collective view of social capital. There was recognition emerging that social capital would contribute to their personal success such as helping to achieve their aspirations and goals. A smaller number referred to social capital being necessary within society at large. This reflects a view of it being something held by a group, not just by individuals, as illustrated in the following:

> *People that are able to make connections with each other and connect people ... are key to making a community and improving communication between people from various backgrounds.*

> *A person cannot achieve much in isolation, we are social beings and need to interact to work towards common goals.*

There was recognition of broader notions of success that can be achieved through collaboration and co-operation between people. As two respondents said:

> *To promote and initiate sustainable global change and influence, you need social capital and help to do it – you can't do it alone. It is as Issac Newton said "I am great because I stand on the shoulders of giants".*

> *Achieving great things together that individuals cannot achieve on their own*

Here, students were acknowledging that communities and societies are characterised by these interactions and relationships.

The student responses show that they see multiple benefits of building and generating their social capital. These benefits span the academic lifecycle, building on what they bring to, as well as what they acquire throughout and beyond HE. The exercise of reflecting on what social capital can do and how it can be acquired in itself has enabled these students to fully explore the value of HE that goes beyond their programme of study.

BENEFITS FOR INSTITUTIONS

This section identifies a number of emerging benefits of social capital for institutions, derived from the HEA's work on this area over a number of years and reinforced through our present analysis of empirical data from students.

- *Social capital highlights partnership between students and their institution*:

  One of the themes emerging from the HEA's work is the importance of mutual action from both students and institutions to build social capital, which in turn depends on collaboration, co-operation and trust. The institution needs to create and make available opportunities within and outside the curriculum to develop social capital, and yet there is an obligation on a student to make use of them. The notion of partnership is fundamental to the development of social capital, acknowledging both the collective and individual capital of institutions and students alike.

- *Social capital emphasises the interconnected nature of learning in HE*: The transformational power of education is harnessed from the collective impact of the many and varied opportunities that are on offer to students. Social capital places a value on those interconnections: the combination of academic, non-academic, social, formal and/or informal experiences; and promotes learning as lifelong and life-wide.

- *Social capital accounts for the multiple impacts of HE*: The student data highlight the impact of social capital as extending beyond HE; it was thus noted that the majority of student responses were future focussed. Within HE, social capital can be developed through the learning environment and wider opportunities in their broadest sense. Society both contributes to the learning community and benefits from social capital.

- *Social capital promotes equity of student opportunity*: For students entering university through non-traditional routes; from low participation neighbourhoods /under-represented groups or those experiencing inequity and discrimination, social capital can provide a vehicle for counteracting deficit-led models and approaches. Whilst access and awareness are fundamental to building social capital, helping students to understand tangible ways they can benefit from social capital now and in the future is key. This requires attention on developing a sense of mutual trust, collaboration and co-operation to ensure social capital – and all students – flourish.

WHY DOES SOCIAL CAPITAL MATTER IN HE?

At a sector level, social capital can be a useful way to explain the value of HE to students and society at a time when perceptions of its value for money are being challenged. With the introduction of tuition fees in some parts of the UK, the sector has sought to articulate value in terms of the increased life-time earnings a graduate could expect relative to a non-graduate. However, this logic came under threat during the financial downturn, when the earnings gap narrowed and new opportunities such as degree apprenticeships further erode the traditional degree's value proposition by offering their own, i.e. 'earn while you learn'.

Social capital can help to redress the balance away from a purely economic, transactional view of the value of HE towards a more nuanced and accurate representation of HE as a vehicle both to increase earnings potential *and* to develop skills, networks and other opportunities to achieve one's potential.

Some institutions now seek to differentiate themselves by explicitly promoting a focus on developing social capital as an aid to student recruitment. This is often seen in graduate outcomes' statements and in university marketing. In this regard, social capital allows institutions to describe the full range of opportunities available to students in a coherent manner, bringing together pastoral support, personal tutoring, enterprise and employability initiatives, and clubs and societies in a single approach, focussed on improving student life chances.

Social capital could be seen as an amorphous concept for students, but the components within it are of immediately recognisable value. The learning gained from the social aspects of HE cannot be underestimated, whether through peers, staff or through the various experiences on offer; opportunities that enable them to explore, challenge, innovate and critique through learning. The student voices represented in this study, through their reflections on social capital, bring to life the very tangible role of HE in transforming their lives and future choices.

REFERENCES

Bourdieu, P. (1986). The forms of capital. In J. Richardson (Ed.), *Handbook of theory and research for the sociology of education* (pp. 241–258). New York, NY: Greenwood.

Bourdieu, P. (1996). *The state nobility*. Cambridge: Polity Press.

Coleman, J. S. (1988). Social capital in the creation of human capital. *American Journal of Sociology*, *94*, 95–120.

Claridge, T. (2004). *Definitions of social capital. Social capital and natural resource management: An important role for social capital?* Unpublished thesis, University of Queensland, Brisbane, Australia. Retrieved from https://www.socialcapitalresearch.com/literature/definition.html. Accessed on November 11, 2017.

Naidoo, R. (2015). *Higher education, social capital and mobility*. York, UK: Higher Education Academy.

Putnam, R. (2000). *Bowling alone*. New York, NY: Simon and Schuster.

7

'SO, YOU WANT TO BE AN ACADEMIC?' THE EXPERIENCES OF BLACK, ASIAN AND MINORITY ETHNIC UNDERGRADUATES IN A UK CREATIVE ARTS UNIVERSITY

Siobhan Clay

ABSTRACT

This case study focusses on student conceptions of becoming an academic, and their perceptions of their institution's role in supporting them, or creating barriers, on this journey. In-depth qualitative research was conducted with nine undergraduate Fine Art and Design students from a range of Black, Asian and Minority Ethnic (BAME) and White backgrounds to understand the impact that tutor relationships; the curriculum, creative pedagogies and the invisibility of diverse teaching staff might have on their journey

*through, and sense of belonging within, the academy.
It is positioned amid the current BAME attainment gap
in UK higher education (HE) and takes as its context
the discourse on the lack of BAME academics in UK
universities; an issue more pronounced in the creative
disciplines (ECU, 2017a, p. 158).*

*The aim of the study was to understand how institutional
practices might support or hinder students returning to
the academy as staff, using Critical-Race Theory and
whiteness and cultural capital frameworks to situate the
research. The findings present an overwhelming interest
amongst the students in teaching as a future career, and
makes a case that students' motivations and aspirations
to teach, if fostered and supported, could partially
remediate the current lack of BAME staff in HE.*

Keywords: Inclusivity; diversity; teaching; access; creative
subjects; higher education

INTRODUCTION

Despite a steady increase in student ethnic diversity across UK
higher education (HE) from 15% Black, Asian and Minority
Ethnic (BAME) students in 2003/4 to 22% in 2015/16 (Equality
Challenge Unit (ECU), 2017b, p. 118), the academic staff demographic remains relatively static, with BAME staff accounting
for just 6.5% of teaching roles in UK HE (ECU, 2017a, p. 69).

The aim of this small-scale case study, undertaken at
a large UK Creative Arts University, was to gain a detailed
understanding of the experiences of diverse students during
their undergraduate journey, and to describe their perceptions
of institutional practices that act as barriers or enablers to
them becoming university teaching staff in the future.

The study consisted of semi-structured interviews with nine students from courses in the discipline areas of Art, Design and Communications that had above 40% BAME students in the second year of study. Five female participants from BAME backgrounds and four from white British or white European backgrounds took part. Each interview lasted between 36 minutes to one hour.

The study follows high-profile campaigns such as *Absent from the Academy* (Richards, 2013) and 'Why isn't my professor black?' (UCLTV, 2014), which focussed on the dearth of UK black Professors: just 85 from a UK total of 18,500. It highlights social justice, equity and equality of opportunity issues in education, and foregrounds implications for social mobility within the UK.

The BAME attainment gap has very real implications for an individual's future career within the Arts. Progression is intrinsically linked to attainment. Postgraduate study generally (and in the Arts) requires a first-class or upper second-class honours degree. Statistically, fewer BAME students achieve these classes of degree, so returning to HE as an academic is harder. This is where social networks and possessing the 'right' cultural capital play an increasingly important role in the journey, which can be more difficult for BAME and Widening Participation (WP) students (Allen, Quinn, Hollingworth, & Rose, 2013).

FURTHER CONTEXT

Despite greater diversity than the UK HE sector as a whole, low BAME teacher numbers in Art and Design subjects are mirrored in the United States (National Centre for Education Statistics, 2017). Kraehe (2015) undertook an ethnographic study of two black female pre-service art and design teachers to understand their experiences within a predominantly white teacher education setting. They recounted experiences of micro aggressions – slights and racial stereotyping – alongside more subtle forms of 'identity undermining' such as an absence of race-conscious course material in the curriculum. Kraehe's study highlighted the gaps in teacher training, which a more critical and inclusive curriculum might ameliorate.

BAME academics account for 5.7% (375) of total staff in UK HE Creative Arts subjects (ECU, 2017, p. 158). Bhopal and Jackson (2013) interviewed 35 BAME HE staff to understand how career trajectories and identities were affected by working in mainly white institutions. Although rarely subject to overt discrimination, staff experienced subtle forms of *difference* such as over-surveillance and a lack of trust in their work compared to their white peers. The research highlights a narrative of having to 'fit in' to academic spaces that require certain modes of language and behaviour, which can compromise someone's sense of cultural identity and 'belonging'.

This echoes Youdell's (2010) research on teacher perceptions of black students in UK schools, which saw strong cultural identities – 'constituted through students' bodily and linguistic practices' (p. 12) – positioned in opposition to the school's rules and expected student behaviour. Such studies illustrate how career and educational success can come at the expense of staff and student cultural identity and, potentially, their well-being: a kind of trade-off when they have to 'act-white' to succeed.

There is a growing understanding of the mechanisms, policies and structures within the UK and the US education systems that operate to the detriment of BAME students (Gillborn, 2013, 2014; Leonardo, 2002). This is evidenced by recent UK statistics (Equalities and Human Rights Commission, 2016) that refute concepts of UK meritocracy and instead illustrate that opportunity in work, education, housing and social mobility is heavily weighted in favour of white citizens.

KEY FINDINGS IN CONTEXT

Lack of Staff Diversity

'They need to increase staff diversity full stop'.

Seeing staff from similar backgrounds was an important factor in confirming that students' choice of subject could lead to viable careers in the industry and/or university. A sense of 'fit and belonging' was closely aligned to positive staff-student relationships with all BAME students discussing the importance of seeing staff who looked like them in their college environments. The visibility of BAME staff engendered a sense of agency, and signalled the means to be successful within the discipline:

> *... but just seeing them there [BAME staff], to me I feel confident in a way, [...] if this person is in this position teaching [...], it means it's very possible and it's very encouraging.*

However, this was an atypical design course and students recognised a predominantly white staff homogeneity. The lack of staff from diverse backgrounds was deeply troubling for some participants:

> *... black people are less featured in fine art, anyway. And then when you see that you're under-represented within the college staff, I just said, most of your black staff are in Estates or they're in admin, so the only place that black people see other black people is in Estates, that's it.*

For others, the lack of visible role models destabilised a sense of belonging in the institution:

> *... in terms of inspiration and kind of, looking up to people, I do think it's important to have people*

that resemble you [...] I haven't seen any black
women, I haven't seen any women who are Muslim,
I haven't seen a diverse range of women.

This aspect of the case-study findings echoes work by Theuri (2015) who, in considering the potential for racism in Arts subjects in UK HE, confirms 'locked-in inequality' that works against BAME students in the curriculum, and in a lack of teacher diversity.

It is important to note that students talked of having successful relationships with staff from different genders, ethnic and class backgrounds to their own; however, this relied on staff possessing characteristics of openness, understanding and inclusive pedagogic practices, which were evident for some but missing for others.

Teaching Career Vaguely Framed

The student participants were deeply motivated with high industry ambitions and aspirations. They used words such as 'heart palpitations', 'passion' and 'love' to describe why they had chosen their subject, with a belief that their course would help them realise personal and career goals. There was unanimous interest in university teaching that was unencumbered by perceived 'barriers', and deficit discourse around the institutions' role in supporting or hindering access was absent.

Personal characteristics such as 'organised' and 'focussed' were mentioned but not race, religion, class or disability as potential obstacles to teaching. However, aside from consensus that a higher level of qualification and industry experience would help, the specifics of securing a teaching role lacked clarity, was vaguely framed, and they called for greater dialogue to make the process more transparent. One unifying point was the perception that staff had been students at the institution and that strong networks supported a return as staff, which could prove difficult for an external candidate to infiltrate:

> *...so it's all, like, they were all bred and brought up here, they grew up here and they know what's required of them, and I'm not sure if they would think of someone outside, unless that person has shown some spectacular skills...*

These findings reinforce those of several other studies. For example,

- Burke and McManus (2009) found the Art and Design admissions process implicitly biased towards white middle-class students, whose cultural and linguistic capital (Bourdieu & Passeron, 1987) was privileged.

- Hatton (2015) describes Art and Design teaching reproducing 'classed' expressions of cultural value and knowledge that work against working-class students.

- Yosso's (2005) concept of *community cultural wealth* holds particular relevance in an art context where identity, cultural background and experiences undoubtedly shape creativity. Yosso argues that diverse students' multilanguage, multi-generational and social-group flexibility are highly valued cultural resources, which should be of benefit, rather than deficit, at university.

- Stevenson (2015) considers how BAME Art and Design students position their 'identity work' in order to 'become' an active participant in the field, and found them having to navigate the process of 'becoming' largely on their own. Stevenson calls for stronger student communities so that those with limited familial knowledge of art and HE can nonetheless share meanings and identities with their peers to gain recognition and grow the field of art and design.

- Clegg (2011) elaborates on this theme to discuss working class and minority ethnic students' over-representation in post-1992 universities and their regular self-exclusion from more elite HEIs or HE altogether. This has the function of 'limiting the cultural capital growth' of some students, affecting future employment opportunities in a neo-liberal marketplace, which favours strong cultural capital over 'good degrees' from less elite institutions (Clegg, 2011, p. 98).

When asked whether her student experience could have a bearing on her experience as a teacher, one student replied:

> ...I think it's obvious that there would be a real lot of politics and dynamics going down within the institution. I think it would just feel like being a student, that the same issues would be, you know, 'how much should I say, how forthright can I be?'

Additionally, one of the students thought the limited diversity within industry had a direct impact on the current staff demographic, but recognised that more students within the subject field could eventually change this:

> ...it's only going to happen once there are enough diverse people in the industry to come back [...] so because there is more diversity now and there are lot more people that are interested in these type of fields, then I think it will be reflected in the staff members when those students come back.

CRITICAL AND REFLECTIVE DISCUSSION

Staff and a White Curriculum

The case study findings echo recent literature on the impact a strong staff-student relationship can have on improving students' sense of belonging and place in their academic community (Mountford-Zimdars et al., 2015). Finding a connection with staff is particularly important in Art and Design where pedagogies of ambiguity (Austerlitz et al., 2008) mean that good staff relationships can help to stabilise students in a discipline that requires constant risk-taking, performance and self-exploration (Stevenson, 2015).

Whilst all participants could see the benefits of greater staff diversity, it was more urgent for some of the BAME students to see staff who reflected them. The lack of diversity in course teams presented comparatively few problems for the white participants, who considered greater diversity an *added* positive, an opportunity to experience culturally rich skills and ways of working that were lacking in the curriculum. Viewed through a 'whiteness lens' (Leonardo, 2002), we could posit that white representation is so prevalent and normalised it is possible that we no longer 'see' or notice its advantage for some, and disadvantage for others (Gillborn, 2014). Additionally, it could be argued that this privileges relationships in what Stevenson (2012) considers white students' double advantage: access to abundant staff *and* peers who are in their likeness.

Aspirations to Teach

The students expressed an interest in teaching as a future career *despite* some challenging experiences. This brought to mind Stevenson's (2012) 'elaborated' or 'feared possible-selves' in which students enact behaviours and strategies that fulfil 'elaborated' or 'feared' identities. For some participants, the lack of affirmation along with difficulties encountered during their studies had not altered their positive conceptions of an 'elaborated future-self'. Instead, they saw the potential to work, and be successful, in the industry and possibly return as teachers.

The interview narratives provided evidence that perceived barriers were largely conceived as character-driven or self-imposed, 'there's only the barriers you create yourself'; and students discussed 'enabling' personal attributes for becoming academic staff such as being focussed, talented and organised. These narratives point to the individual as determinant of success rather than a consideration of institutional barriers that we know impact upon BAME staff's presence in HE (Bhopal & Jackson, 2013).

The students who were keen to find out more, that is, 'that this could actually be a job', saw the lack of discourse about teaching as a missed opportunity. This narrative 'gap' strongly connects to pedagogies of ambiguity (Austerlitz et al., 2008) as the lack of explicit 'becoming a tutor' discourse, perpetuates the mystery and vagary of Art and Design subjects and industry. It makes transitioning through the system and into the field, a potentially fraught and largely unsupported journey.

Within Art and Design HE, there is a common perception that alumni become staff through informal networks and connections, which strongly privilege white, middle-class students. This is evident in data that show a decrease in BAME Art and Design staff despite increasing BAME student numbers (at the researched university). Critical Race Theory scholars (e.g., Gillborn, 2013) would argue that such informality and vaguely framed progression processes are structural actions, which preserve and legitimise the institution's white hegemony. This was clearly 'seen' by the participants in the university environment.

Finally, the lack of discourse about teaching makes several implicit assumptions. First, that students will naturally transition to industry, gain experience and build successful networks to one day return as staff. Second, that they will attain a 'good' degree (first-class or upper second-class honours) to support them on this journey. Both assumptions ignore the fact that

BAME creative practitioners are underrepresented in the industry, accounting for just 11.4% of the workforce (Creative Industries Federation, 2015) and, additionally, that the current UK BAME attainment gap may act as a significant barrier to continued study or work in such a highly competitive sector.

CONCLUSION

This research provides evidence that BAME students 'see' their lack of visibility in the academy. The study underlines a moral imperative to increase recruitment of BAME staff across the sector. It highlights an interest in HE teaching as a future career; particularly, for students underrepresented in the field. The findings also point to a perception that staff were often alumni of the institution and that some students are favoured over others. This suggests strongly that we need to question who has access to informal opportunities that lead to teaching roles, who is left out and why.

These findings echo literature on the experiences of a diversity of students in UK HE. It is evident that, regardless of discipline, students from BAME backgrounds can experience limited acknowledgement, support and representation within the academy. However, it is also clear that having a supportive relationship with just one member of staff who is open, curious about their work, life and interests, understanding and inclusive, could largely mitigate the current lack of teacher diversity and visibility.

If the sector is serious about solving the persistent BAME attainment gap and dearth of BAME academics in UK HE, we must take a critical look at current institutional and pedagogic practices that can act as barriers to success and teaching as a career. Crucially, we must engage in more honest and respectful discourse with our diverse student body.

REFERENCES

Allen, K., Quinn, J., Hollingworth, S., & Rose, A. (2013). Becoming employable students and 'ideal' creative workers: Exclusion and inequality in higher education work placements. *British Journal of Sociology of Education*, *34*(3), 431–452. doi:doi.org/10.1080/01425692.2012.714249

Austerlitz, N., Blythman, M., Jones, B. A., Jones, C. A., Grove-White, A., Morgan, S. J., … Vaughan, S. (2008). Mind the gap: Expectations, ambiguity and pedagogy within art and design higher education. In L. Drew (Ed.). *The student experience in art and design higher education: Drivers for change* (pp. 125–148). Cambridge: GLAD.

Bhopal, K., & Jackson, J. (2013). *The experiences of black and minority ethnic academics: Multiple identities and career progression* (p. 29). University of Southampton. Retrieved from https://eprints.soton.ac.uk/350967/. Accessed on February 21, 2018.

Bourdieu, P., & Passeron, J.-C. (1977). *Reproduction in education, society and culture*. London: Sage.

Burke, P.-J., & McManus, J. (2009). *Art for a few: Exclusion and misrecognition in art and design higher education admissions*. London: NALN Research Report. Retrieved from https://www.heacademy.ac.uk/system/files/naln_art_for_a_few.pdf

Clegg, S. (2011). Cultural capital and agency: Connecting critique and curriculum in higher education. *British Journal of Sociology of Education*, *32*(1), 93–108.

Creative Industries Federation (CIF). (2015). Creative diversity: The state of diversity in the UK's creative industries and what we can do about it. Retrieved from https://www.creativeindustriesfederation.com/sites/

default/files/2017-06/30183-CIF%20Access%20&%20 Diversity%20Booklet_A4_Web%20(1)(1).pdf. Accessed on February 27, 2018

Equality Challenge Unit (ECU). (2017). Equality in Higher Education Staff (a) and Students (b) Statistical Report 2017. Retrieved from https://www.ecu.ac.uk/publications/ equality-in-higher-education-statistical-report-2017/

Equalities and Human Rights Commission. (2016). Healing a Divided Britain: The Need for Comprehensive Race Equality Strategy. Retrieved from https://www. equalityhumanrights.com/sites/default/files/healing_ a_divided_britain_-_the_need_for_a_comprehensive_ race_equality_strategy_final.pdf. Accessed on February 28, 2018.

Equality Challenge Unit (ECU). (2017b). Equality in Higher Education Students Statistical Report 2017. Retrieved from https://www.ecu.ac.uk/publications/ equality-in-highereducation-statistical-report-2017/

Gillborn, D. (2013). Interest divergence and the colour of cutbacks: Race, recession and the undeclared war on black children. *Discourse: Studies in the Cultural Politics of Education*, 34(4), 477–491.

Gillborn, D. (2014). Racism as policy: A critical race analysis of education reforms in the United States and England. *The Educational Forum*, 78(1), 26–41.

Hatton, K. (2015). *Towards an inclusive arts education*. London: IOE Press.

Kraehe, A. M. (2015). Sounds of silence: Race and emergent counter-narratives of art teacher identity. *The National Art Education Association Studies in Art Education*, 56(3),

199–213. doi: http://www.tandfonline.com/doi/abs/10. 1080/00393541.2015.11518963

Leonardo, Z. (2002). The souls of white folk: Critical pedagogy, whiteness studies, and globalization discourse. *Race Ethnicity and Education.* 5(1), 29–50. doi:https://doi. org/10.1080/13613320120117180

Mountford-Zimdars, A., Sabri, D., Moore, J., Sanders, J., Jones, S., & Higham, L. (2015). Causes of Differences in Student Outcomes, HEFCE. Retrieved from http://dera. ioe.ac.uk/23653/1/HEFCE2015_diffout.pdf. Accessed on February 28, 2018.

National Centre for Education Statistics. (2017). Retrieved from https://nces.ed.gov/fastfacts/display.asp?id=61. Accessed on March 1, 2018.

Richards, N. E. (2013). (March 1, 2018). Absent from the Academy: The lack of Black Academics in the UK Limits the Wider Impact of Universities. Retrieved from http://blogs.lse. ac.uk/impactofsocialsciences/2013/11/06/absent-from-the-academy/. Accessed on March 1, 2018.

Stevenson, J. (2012). An exploration of the link between minority ethnic and white students degree attainment and views of their future possible selves. *Higher Education Studies,* 2(4). 103–113. doi:doi.org/10.5539/hes.v2n4p103

Stevenson, C. (2015). Identity, research and the arts curriculum: Counterstorytelling as academic practice. In K. Hatton (Ed.), *Towards an inclusive arts education* (pp. 119–137). London: IOE Press.

Theuri, S. (2015). Critical race theory and its relationship to art education. In K. Hatton, (Ed.), *Towards an inclusive arts education* (pp. 59–77). London: IOE Press.

UCLTV. (2014). Why isn't my Professor Black? UCL Panel Discussion. Retrieved from https://www.youtube.com/watch?v=mBqgLK9dTk4. Accessed on March 1, 2018.

Yosso, T. J. (2005). Whose culture has capital? A critical race theory discussion of community cultural wealth. *Race Ethnicity & Education*, 8(1), 69–91. doi: https://doi.org/10.1080/1361332052000341006

Youdell, D. (2010). Identity traps or how black students fail: The interactions between biographical, sub-cultural, and learner identities. *British Journal of Sociology of Education*, 24, 4–20. doi: https://doi.org/10.1080/01425690301912

8

STUDENTS' VIEWS OF TERTIARY EDUCATION AS 'ACCESS TO SUCCESS': A CASE STUDY OF A MULTICULTURAL COLLEGE IN ISRAEL

Bruria Schaedel

ABSTRACT

This study examines students' views of the institutional learning environments, which add to their academic and social success, in a multicultural college. The relationships between the students' background characteristics and their academic skills, self-efficacy and interactions with the academic and administrative staff are analysed utilising quantitative and qualitative methods. The findings indicate that the students encounter difficulties in their academic studies because of low attainment in academic literacy. However, students with higher self-efficacy actively seek assistance to advance their academic skills, whilst students with lower self-efficacy circumvent academic-assistance resources available on campus. Nonetheless, most students are motivated to succeed in their academic studies and continue them further.

The study concludes with recommendations for future measures to enhance students' self-efficacy and the specific needs of students of diverse ethnic and national origin.

Keywords: Higher education; learning environments; self-efficacy

INTRODUCTION AND CONTEXT

Until the 1990s, the gates of the eight elite research universities in Israel were closed to many students because of stringent selective requirements of high matriculation and Scholastic Assessment Test (SAT) achievements (Ayalon & Yogev, 2005). Yet, economic and social pressures for increased access and equality for marginalised groups to participate in higher education institutions (HEI) resulted in the Council for Higher Education's (CHE) decision to increase enrolment to HEI, adding private and regional public colleges. The colleges awarded bachelor's degrees equivalent to university bachelor degrees and granted less selective entrance requirements. The private colleges offer studies in fields such as: law, business administration, economics, engineering and management. They are located mainly in the central part of Israel. Their tuition fees are three times higher than the universities and the public colleges. The public colleges were built in the geographic periphery of the country and offer studies in education, social studies and humanities. Their tuition fees are subsidised by the CHE and private agencies.

This transformation has been paralleled by dramatically increasing rates of student enrolment in HE; particularly, in the colleges, and especially of underrepresented groups: women, those from lower socio-economic status (SES) backgrounds, newcomers and Arab minorities. By 2016–2017, 66% of the 20–25 years' age group were enrolled in HE. Amongst Jewish students, 68% are female and 20% are newcomers from the Former Soviet Union (FSU) and 1.2% from Ethiopia. The Arab minority students include 15% Muslims, Christian and Druze (of whom 67% are female) (Central Bureau of Statistics, 2017).

Yet, the increased access to HE led to stratification of, and inequality within, the system (Feniger & Ayalon, 2013). Students with lower matriculation and SAT achievements and those of low SES, particularly from the geographic periphery, did not enrol in the private colleges because of the high tuition fees and the far distance of them from their homes. Students from higher SES with higher entrance achievements enrol in the universities and private colleges and choose subjects that eventually lead to higher SES. Equally, male students elect science, engineering and computer studies, whilst female students elect to study law, administration, social studies and education (Feniger & Ayalon, 2013).

Whatever be these patterns of admissions, students from the geographic periphery who enrol in public regional colleges encounter many obstacles. Because of the low entrance matriculation diploma and SAT achievements, the literacy attainments of Jewish students in Hebrew, English and mathematics are poor (Rach, 2006). Amongst the Arab students, this is even more substantial, because Hebrew is their second language. Most of them are first generation in HE and often struggle with adjustment to the college learning environment (LE) and the burden of high financial expenditure (Feniger & Ayalon, 2013).

The widespread access of previously under-represented students to the public colleges poses new challenges for teachers, students and the quality of the college environment, which is instrumental in fostering student academic proficiencies for successful graduation with a bachelor's degree.

Relevant research and related literature suggest that student success in college is based on a LE that supports their academic and personal development; acquiring academic and communication competencies such as critical thinking, academic literacy and the ability to work effectively with others.

LE is fundamental in shaping the academic, interpersonal and extracurricular activities that facilitate students' success and the teaching, learning approaches and organisation of their resources (Pike & Kuh, 2006). This entails a shift from an emphasis on teaching to one on student learning; for example, using classroom experiences that stimulate learning (Kezar & Kinzie, 2006) and support interaction with administrators, faculty advisors, internship supervisors, mentors and 'out-of-class experiences'.

LE includes pedagogical support services, and learning how to use on-campus learning resources, manage time, set goals, study for tests and how to access learning technologies (Barefoot, 2008). According to attitude-behaviour and social cognitive theories (Kandiko & Mawer, 2013), self-efficacy – as a key element of social cognitive theory – is a significant variable in student learning, affecting bothmotivation and learning. Social cognitive theory considers internal personal factors of student performance and learning behaviour, such as tasks they choose, their effort, perseverance and performances (Schunk, 2003). Self-efficacy helps students to persevere when faced with academic and social challenges, whilst those who are less confident are more likely to fail when encountering difficult situations (Van Dinther, Dochy, & Segres, 2011).

Cultural perspective theory suggests that many traditionally underrepresented minority groups encounter challenges when they reach college. First-generation students pursuing HE have less implicit knowledge about college, are less prepared for dealing with the challenges and find it difficult to perform well academically and to adjust socially (Gofen, 2007). Low SES students face difficulties like those of first-generation students; in addition, their families lack the resources and social capital necessary to support their success in college (Perna & Titus, 2005).

The present case study postulated that students' views of their LE affect their motivation to succeed in their present and future studies. The study wanted to examine in what ways students' perceptions of LE are related to self-assessment of self-efficacy, and to age, ethnic/national origins and academic proficiencies.

THE CASE STUDY

The Participants — General

The sample composed 656 students from a small public college located in the northern periphery of Israel. Most respondents, 511 (80%), were females and 125 (20%) were males.[1] Almost half (40%) of the students study education, 40% social studies, 6.3% economics and 5.4% political science. Nearly half of the students are Jewish (45%), the majority of whom were born in Israel; 9% are immigrants from the FSU and Ethiopia. Of the Arab students (55% of the sample), 36% were Muslim and 9% Christian and Druze.

---

1 Twenty participants did not answer this question.

The average age of the Jewish students ranged between 23 and 26 years, whilst the average age of the Arab students was 18–21.[2] In terms of the subjects being studied, these are:

- 40% education,

- 40% social studies,

- 6% economics,

- 5% political science and

- 9% criminology.

Most of the students reside in small towns and rural villages near the college. Many (80%) live with their parents, and 20% have their own families. Over half of the Jewish and Arab students (54%) are first generation in HE. Most of the Jewish students (87%), and less than half (40%) of the Arab students, are employed in part-time jobs (between 10 and 20 hours per week).

Social, Economic and Educational Background

The entrance scores of the Jewish students in the matriculation test were 81 (from a total of 100) and the average SAT score is 535 (out of 800). These scores are higher than the average matriculation scores of the Arab students, which were 76 and 480, respectively. The national average matriculation score for enrolment in an HEI is 75 and 573 in the SAT exam.[3]

---

2 It is worth noting that Jewish male and female adults who are 18 years old are required to serve for two to three years mandatory army duty, while the great majority of Arab students, who are exempt from army duty, enroll in HE at the age of 18.

3 Entrance requirements for studies such as medicine, computing and engineering require higher test results.

The great majority of the students are from lower SES background. Few of the Jewish parents (20%) possess an academic degree, and the Arab parents fewer still. Amongst the Arab mothers, the Christian mothers are more highly educated than the Muslim and Druze mothers. However, few of the mothers (21%) hold professional jobs (nurse and teacher), the rest have blue-collar jobs, or are 'housewives'. Many of the fathers are employed in blue-collar jobs in various industries. The average income of Jewish families is low, and amongst the Arabs even lower (Central Bureau of Statistics, 2017).

Typically, the Jewish families include four to five people, whilst the Muslim and Druze families include six to nine people. Many students qualify for subsidised aid for their college tuition fees, which they receive from the CHE and private agencies. However, most Arab families (84%) finance almost all their children's academic expenditure, whilst Jewish families finance about half (58%) of the remaining tuition, because many of their children hold part-time jobs.

Generally, the students at the College represent the multicultural, lower SES composition of the population in the northern geographic periphery of Israel. The close proximity of the college to students' homes enables many students (men and women) to pursue their academic studies regardless of their job and family obligations. The students' families willingly assist their children's college expenditures, because they regard the tertiary education of their children as highly important regardless of their limited resources.

The Focus of the Study

Student views regarding their LE and self-efficacy were obtained using a questionnaire that included: students' demographic characteristics, their views of the college learning and social experiences as well as their aspirations for future study.

The students assigned the utmost importance to the following factors and skills that contribute to their academic success.

Skills needed for academic success. Taking tests, note-taking, reading, being aware of one's individual learning style, time management, memory techniques and interactions with academic faculty who care about student learning and success.

The Jewish students attribute greater importance to these skills than the Arab students for their academic success.

Literacy and communication skills. Many of the Jewish and Arab students regard skills such as: writing, reading, oral communication skills and effective strategies to increase comprehension and retention of information, as important for their success. However, students who obtained higher scores in the matriculation and the SAT examinations did not find these items important for their academic success.

Academic learning assistance and support services. Students regarded familiarity with the campus and academic resources, including assistance with academic and personal guidance and technology, as crucial. Many (see the following) also regarded prompt feedback about their learning assignments as equally important.

The Jewish students assign more importance to the quality of interactions with the academic and administrative staff than Arab students, and they preferred prompt feedback on their performance.

Persistence. These items refer to the ability to set and pursue intermediate and long-term goals. Jewish students displayed a higher capacity to cope with, and overcome, obstacles compared to the Arab students.

Learning in Small Groups. The Jewish students assigned greater importance to studying in small, intimate and groups with their peers compared to the Arabs students.

STUDENTS' SELF-EFFICACY

Self-efficacy influences the choices students make, the efforts they exert, and the persistence and resilience they apply when confronted with difficulties. The self-efficacy scale includes 10 items. Correlations scores for each item (α = 0.86) are high for all participants. This indicates that all the respondents possess the inner resources and confidence to make the extra effort to achieve the goals they set out for themselves.

However, the Jewish students' scores are significantly higher than the Arab students'. The Jewish students have greater confidence in their ability to cope with difficult situations and believe they will succeed in their studies, whilst the Arab students lack confidence in their ability to succeed.

The background variables that contribute to the higher self-efficacy of the Jewish students are: high matriculation and SAT achievements; being part-time employed during their studies in college; their motivation to succeed and perseverance to overcome obstacles. Most of them gained experience that helped them to persist and overcome academic and financial challenges during their academic studies, during their service to the army.

The main difficulties that most students encounter are with written and oral language assignments. Many respondents maintained that they exert far more effort and time to succeed in their present studies at college than in high school. Many students desired additional tutorials in higher quality language proficiencies and written academic assignments. The Arab students would like more personal assistance from the academic, administrative staff and the library services. In addition, they would want better interpersonal interactions with the academic and administrative counsellors.

The students maintained that their main reason for enrolling in the college was the proximity to their homes and their belief that the academic degree would help their economic and social advancement. Irrespective of their difficulties, many of the students are very motivated to succeed in their studies. The Muslim students displayed the highest motivation to succeed in their present studies, followed by the Jewish, the Druze and Christian-Arab students.

Many students plan to continue further studies at university for a graduate degree in social work or at a teacher-training college to obtain a teaching diploma (the College does not offer these studies). Nearly half of the Arab students wished to continue their studies for graduate degrees at university or at a teacher training college, whilst a third of the Jewish students intended to continue their academic education.

WHAT DID WE FIND AND WHAT DOES IT MEAN?

Students of the periphery encounter many learning, social and financial barriers upon their access to HE. The main obstacle is low levels of language and learning proficiencies that stem from the lower quality of the primary and secondary educational systems in the northern geographical regions in comparison to higher learning proficiencies and matriculation achievements of secondary schools in affluent regions and communities in the centre of the country. This gap also persists in teachers' qualifications and teaching methods, and students' choices of studying maths and sciences in high school.

According to the social cognitive theories, students' lower self-efficacy derives from repeated strong 'negative mastery experiences' in elementary and secondary education, where teachers focus on retention rather than on competencies mastered, which leads to decreasing levels of self-efficacy and low assessment (Van Dinther, Mochy, & Segers, 2011).

The Jewish students with higher self-efficacy assessments are determined to overcome their insufficiencies by active participation in the various learning supports that are available on campus. They assign high importance to learning proficiencies of written academic assignments, time-management skills and methods to succeed in test taking. According to attitude-behaviour and self-efficacy theories, students with high self-efficacy overcome complications by seeking help from academic and administrative staff on campus. Student–faculty interactions have a multidimensional influence on cognitive and social growth as well as academic performance.

The Arab students, who also regard academic literacy as essential for success in their academic studies, are disinclined to get the assistance needed to improve their lower attainments needed for academic success. They avoid interactions with the academic and other support staff, such as advisors and tutors, and do not attend supportive instructional programmes. They do not regard studying in small classes as important, and they see no need to improve the skills that facilitate learning success, such as time-management skills and taking tests. Perhaps, their low self-efficacy prevents them from actively pursuing the academic support measures that they need.

According to the cultural perspective theory, minority groups circumvent the use of campus-learning support resources because of their feeling of estrangement and mistrust of the faculty, staff and administrators (Barefoot, 2008). Arar, Harzalla-Masry, and Haj-Yehia (2013) maintain that the Arab students do not seek the support services on campus because of the western orientation of the college climate, which is new to them.

Being 'first generation in college' is also a major source of difficulty for the Jewish and Arab students. Students may have difficulties in getting used to administrative and curriculum requirements and making decisions regarding course choices. For the first-generation Arab students, these are even greater difficulties. Abu-Saad (2006) found that 40% of the Arab students change their field of study after their first year in college because of unfamiliarity with the diverse fields of study and lack of knowledge of the job market.

Yet, interestingly, first-generation students in college get financial and emotional support from their families, who are willing to make substantial sacrifices for their children to suc- ceed in their tertiary education. Their families capitalise on their social capital, social resilience and their human and cultural capital within the family to help their children to overcome the difficulties (Perna & Titus, 2005). Gofen (2007) found that parental educational aspirations of lower income families in Israel were for their first-generation children to break the inter- generational poverty cycle by acquiring a bachelor's degree.

Irrespective of their hardships, the students are highly motivated to pursue their college education successfully. The Arab and Jewish students are highly motivated to success- fully advance their study in the college and continue to study after their graduation in universities and teacher colleges that offer a teaching certificate. For many Arab women, the close proximity of the college to their communities allows them to acquire an academic degree because religious rules would not favour long hours of travel to a college in the centre. Since 2005, the proportion of the female Arab students has surpassed the proportion of male students (Arar, Harzalla- Masry, & Haj-Yehia, 2013).

CONCLUSIONS AND RECOMMENDATIONS

The 'colleges in the periphery' offer access to tertiary edu- cation for under-represented groups of the Jewish and Arab students, adding to their economic and social capital because of the academic education, and other learning opportunities, they have in the college.

We recommend that colleges in the periphery augment their academic, social and financial-support services by joint efforts of the academic and administrative staff to improve the learning and egalitarian climate on campus. The classroom climate should entail a rigorous approach of frequent self-reflection and peer assessment as well as performing tasks that involve constructive conflicts or controversy within teams of students.

The College should employ more Arab administrative, academic and support staff. Faculties and other agents on the campus should initiate multicultural social and academic extracurricular encounters to help the under-represented students overcome their mistrust.

There are some limitations in the scale and scope of this study. It is hoped that future research will address them. The sample was relatively small and based on only one institution. Future research could incorporate data from several HEI and a wider geographic range across the country, as well as seeking the views of administrative and academic staff.

Nevertheless, the present study reveals some very important aspects to the ways in which social, economic, educational, ethnic and geographical factors combine to create complex learning contexts and the implications these have for institutional, student-facing, policies and practices.

REFERENCES

Abu-Saad, I. (2006). *Access to higher education and its socio-economic impact among Bedouin Arabs in Southern Israel*. Israel: Ben-Gurion University. Unpublished data.

Arar, K., Harzalla-Masry, A., & Haj-Yehia, K. (2013). Higher education for Palestinian Muslim female students in Israel and Jordan: Migration and identity formation. *Cambridge Journal of Education*, *43*(1), 51–67.

Ayalon, H., & Yogev, A. (2005). Field of study and students' satisfaction in expended system of higher education: The case of Israel. *European Sociological Review*, *3*, 227–241.

Barefoot, B. (Ed). (2008). The first year and beyond: Rethinking the challenge of collegiate transition. In *New directions for higher education* (p. 44). San Francisco, CA: Jossey-Bass.

Central Bureau of Statistics. (2017). Retrieved from http://www.CBC.Gov.il.

Feniger, Y., & Ayalon, H. (2016). English as gatekeeper: Inequality between Jews and Arabs in access to higher education in Israel. *International Journal of Educational Research*, *76*, 104–111.

Gofen, A. (2007). *Family capital: How first-generation higher-education students break the intergenerational cycle*. Retrieved from http://www.irp.wisc.edu.

Kandiko, C. B., & Mawer, M. (2013). *Student expectations and perceptions of higher education*. London: King's Learning Institute.

Kezar, A., & Kinzie, J. (2006). Examining the ways institutions create student engagement: The role of mission. *Journal of College Student Development*, *47*(2), 149–172.

Perna, L. W., & Titus, M. A. (2005). The relationship between parental involvement as social capital and college enrollment: An examination of racial/ethnic group differences. *Journal of Higher Education*, *76*(5), 485–518.

Pike, G. R., & Kuh, G. D. (2006). Another look at the relationships among structural diversity, informal peer interactions and perceptions of the campus environment. *The Review of Higher Education, 29*(4), 425-450.

Schunk, D. H. (2003). Self-efficacy for reading and writing: Influence of modeling, goal setting and self-evaluation. *Reading and Writing Quarterly: Overcoming Learning Difficulties, 19*(2), 159–172.

Van Dinther, K., Mochy. F., & Segers, M. (2011). Factors affecting students' self-efficacy in higher education. *Educational Research Review, 6*(2), 95–108.

9

COLLECTIVE RESPONSIBILITY AND COLLABORATIVE ACTION: UNIVERSITIES AND EMPLOYERS IN PURSUIT OF SOCIAL MOBILITY

Nik Miller

ABSTRACT

The correlation between social background, and future educational and occupational outcomes, is strengthening in the UK. It is getting harder to ignore the implications, as they manifest themselves in our economic and political fabric. Even when talented young people overcome barriers at a particular stage of their journey to the workplace, new barriers present themselves at the next. For example, it has been assumed historically that gaining access to university has a levelling effect: once you are in, you will get ahead. This is a myth. Those, for whom the cost of higher education

is most significant, often benefit the least. This chapter
explores why this is currently the case, and what can be
done to narrow the gap in graduate outcomes by socio-
economic background.

Keywords: Socio-economic background; retention; employers;
graduate outcomes

INTRODUCTION: THE DEFINING SOCIAL POLICY ISSUE FOR UNIVERSITIES AND OUR TIME

Debate in the UK about social mobility rages on. The gap
between the wealthy and the poor is widening, and those
without the advantages of affluence appear discontent or dis-
engaged. Influence in politics, the media, business and culture is considered the property of the elite, and public trust
in government, business, media and charitable organisations
experienced it's largest-ever decline in 2017 (Edelman, 2017).

Universities in the UK are sometimes celebrated as bastions
of social equality, and have been largely immune from public
distrust. However, fuelled by the overwhelming public sentiment that globalisation has benefitted the few at the expense of
the many, the mood about universities appears to be changing.
Higher education (HE) confers social, cultural and economic
benefits on individuals, and is the gateway to most high-status
professions (Universities UK, 2015). UK graduates are more
likely to be employed than non-graduates are, and their long-
term employment prospects remain strong (UK CES, 2016).
However, university places continue to be accessed disproportionately by those having backgrounds that are more affluent.
In an attempt to address this, vast amounts of resource have
been expended on interventions aimed at enabling a more
diverse group of students to benefit from HE.

This focus on diversifying university admissions is welcome; however, it has only been moderately effective, despite the positive (though inconsistent) introduction of 'foundation years', contextual admissions (see, e.g. Sundorph, Vasilev, & Coiffait in this volume, Chapter 2), and a greater understanding about the need to focus on unequal attainment in schools. More fundamentally, there has not been a correspondingly attentive focus on the experiences of students once they are part of our HE community, and how participation benefits students differentially by socio-economic background (for discussions of closely related questions, see Clay, Chapter 2; May & Jones, Chapter 6; and Thomas, Chapter 14, in this volume). Higher tuition fees, new evidence and a more discriminating sense of value amongst students have all sharpened this focus on graduate outcomes.

THE GAP IN GRADUATE OUTCOMES BY SOCIO-ECONOMIC BACKGROUND

It has been assumed historically that admission to HE has a social-levelling effect. However, the evidence shows otherwise: in the UK, those for whom the cost of HE is most acute often benefit the least. Based on a simple measure of income, students from higher socio-economic backgrounds have median earnings, which are around 25% more compared to those from lower income families controlling for institution type and subject, this premium is preserved at 10% (Institute for Fiscal Studies (IFS), 2017).

This analysis might be considered reductive, because of its sole focus on graduate pay. However, this exposition of the socio-economic pay gap should alarm all of those with an interest in equality. For example, further studies have revealed that when controlling for a wide range of background factors, those from the lowest socio-economic backgrounds are 11% less likely to be in professional employment than those from the most advantaged backgrounds (Higher Education Funding Council for England (HEFCE), 2016).

The narrative that widening university participation is necessary, but not sufficient, has become more prevalent. It is reflected in the 2016 Higher Education White Paper, and in the latest distribution of institutional Access Agreement spending. Considering this latter area, it is projected that in 2020, almost a third of institutional Access Agreement expenditure will be dedicated to student success and progression, compared to the equivalent figure of 15.9% in 2013 (Office for Fair Access (OFFA), 2017). However, despite the increasing proportion of funding dedicated to promoting more equal-graduate outcomes, relatively little is understood about how this funding can be directed most effectively.

FACTORS AFFECTING THE GAP

A complex mix of factors interweaves to drive unequal graduate outcomes. Students' experiences of careers education prior to university are formative, and achieving a quick and comfortable transition to university also plays an important role in graduate outcomes. Then, students from lower socio-economic backgrounds typically participate in fewer activities that have greatest currency amongst employers. These include extra-curricular activities (e.g. leadership roles in sports and societies); internships; international opportunities to study and work and postgraduate education (see, e.g. May & Jones in this volume, Chapter 6). The marketing and selection practices of employers can be supportive, or deeply unhelpful, in widening opportunities for talented students from lower socio-economic groups. Much positive progress is being made, but only by a modest number of employers.

Pre-University Experiences

Schools have been legally responsible for pupils' careers education since 2012. Numerous reports highlight that provision in England is a postcode lottery, with quality varying considerably by school and area. Gaining access to quality careers education is undoubtedly connected to background: a recent survey of students revealed that

> *wealthier students, who were found to have higher social capital, were nearly one and a half times more likely to receive careers education compared with students with lower social capital, who were significantly more likely to be from poorer families. (Social Mobility Commission (SMC), 2016, p. 73)*

The lack of funding to support careers education has also been identified as problematic; this has been found to compound inequality, a dynamic that is often most serious in rural and coastal areas (Bridge Group (BG), 2017a, 2017b).

Careers education at school matters. It has been shown to have positive outcomes on attainment (consistently, the strongest predictor of university participation), and is shown to help young people to better understand the relationship between educational goals and occupational outcomes, thereby increasing pupil motivation (Hooley, Johnson, & Neary, 2016). Overall, students have an advantage in developing their career capability at university if they:

- attended schools with a strong approach to careers education;

- have a family network where careers thinking and planning is accorded high value; and

- have a proactive and confident approach in seeking information and opportunities.

Transition and Retention

An ability to make the transition to university quickly and with little struggle is increasingly important in HE. Employers are typically seeking talent earlier – exemplified by the rise of the first-year internship. Participation in extra-curricular activities is strongly predicted by engagement in the opening term; and the majority of students who drop out of HE do so in the early stages of their studies.

Pupils from lower socio-economic backgrounds are not only considerably less likely to go to university, they are also less likely to complete their degrees if they do make it (IFS, 2014). Retention rates at UK universities are highly favourable compared to most other countries, but the difference in completion rates amongst students from higher and lower socio-economic backgrounds is of concern, including at some of the UK's most prestigious institutions (SMC, 2016). Almost half of the difference in retention rates between these groups is due to socio-economic background, rather than prior attainment or other factors correlated with poor university performance (IFS, 2014). Knowledge of the broad patterns associated with retention is growing, but little is known about how this is differentiated by discipline. The issue is also underexplored at postgraduate level, and the voice of those who do not complete their studies is silent in the majority of research on retention.

Gaining Currency in the Employment Market

The skills and knowledge acquired during university study, but not necessarily through formal learning, impact on graduate outcomes. Students from lower socio-economic backgrounds are less likely to participate in extra-curricular activities, relevant work experience and opportunities to work or study abroad (Trendence, 2018). This is emerging as a primary factor affecting differential graduate outcomes (Bradley & Ingram, 2013; May & Jones in this volume, Chapter 6).

Recent studies indicate that these differences are largely due to a combination of individual student characteristics and preferences, the opportunities available at the institution attended and the role of family and professional networks (Futuretrack, 2013). There is also a geographically uneven distribution of work experience opportunities, with the majority being based in London and the South East. A recent survey showed that 62% of businesses in London had employed an intern, compared to 28% of businesses in the Midlands and 33% in the North (ACCA, Intern Aware and YouGov, 2015). Given the value attributed to work experience by employers, we should be more concerned about the accessibility of such experiences to all students.

Amongst the largest UK employers, around a third of graduate positions are filled by students who have already worked within the organisation through an internship or placement (Association of Graduate Recruiters (AGR), 2016a, 2017b). Internships are increasingly being undertaken during a students' first year of study, and the extent to which these experiences are accessible to all students, regardless of background, is an issue that remains to be explored in sufficient detail. Alongside concerns that unpaid internships contribute to unequal access, there is also a growing concern about the prevalence of unadvertised internships.

There is much evidence to indicate that work and study opportunities overseas offer a significant boost to students' employability. For example, a study on the impact of the Erasmus student exchange programme found that graduates with international experience were significantly more successful in the job market (UK Higher Education International Unit (UKHEIU), 2015). Access to these opportunities is too often the preserve of the privileged: the study also highlights that participation rates in international mobility opportunities are heavily skewed in the favour of students from higher socio-economic backgrounds.

Relatively few studies have focused on the critical roles and responsibilities of university careers services in supporting equal graduate outcomes. Across much of the sector, the resourcing of careers services lags behind the increased importance of the profession (BG, 2017a, 2017b). The use of career services by students is modest and, though there is limited data available, there is some evidence to suggest that engagement affects career outcomes (Futuretrack, 2013). Furthermore, students from lower socio-economic backgrounds are more likely to draw on informal sources for advice, such as websites, and are less likely to access more formal careers provision (AGCAS, 2013).

Employer Practices

Graduate employers in the UK have become much more focused on socio-economic diversity in recent years, driven mainly by:

- a desire to access a wider talent pool;
- pressure from peer organisations and the media, fuelled by initiatives such as the Social Mobility Employer Index;

- an increasingly dependable evidence base about effective practices; and

- an emerging business case for socio-economic diversity, built on the relationship between diversity and organisational performance.

However, many of the elite professions are still less representative when compared to the least diverse universities. Recent data show, for example, that 4% of doctors, 6% of barristers and 11% of journalists are from lower socio-economic backgrounds (Laurison & Friedman, 2015; see also Sundorph, Vasilev, & Coiffait in this volume, Chapter 2).

However, amongst large employers, marketing, recruitment and selection activities typically compound one another, with the overall effect of advantaging those from higher socio-economic backgrounds (BG, 2016a). Around a quarter of employers monitor socio-economic diversity amongst their graduate intake; whereas, a higher proportion have specific strategies to address it (AGR, 2016a, 2016b). This work is typically embryonic. Many employers are endeavouring to address socio-economic diversity without a sufficient understanding of the scale of the problem they face, how to achieve the greatest impact in tackling it, or how then to evaluate the impact achieved.

Lack of diversity in the professions is a construct of supply (the pipeline of applicants) and demand – the selection and recruitment practices of employers. UK universities with lower levels of socio-economic diversity, across their student bodies, receive on average many more visits from top employers (SMC, 2017). Whilst the institution attended by a student may in some ways reflect ability, it also encodes unfair advantage to students from higher socio-economic backgrounds. Students at the most selective universities, on average, have greater opportunity to develop social capital (see, e.g. May &

Jones in this volume, Chapter 6) by accessing more support on their journey to university, having wider social networks and enjoying more careers support.

By favouring students who have had disproportionate access to these advantages, many employers are overlooking talented candidates who could perform exceptionally, given the opportunity. Many students educated at non-selective state schools also self-select out of the application process in relatively high numbers, on the basis that they feel they will not 'fit-in' or their academic credentials will not prove strong enough. For example, a recent study into socio-economic diversity in the Civil Service Fast Stream revealed that many candidates found the recruitment process "attractive but intimidating" (BG, 2016b).

Beyond marketing, the way in which employers define talent and, in turn, the way in which this informs selection processes, is critical. Candidate screening criteria are a significant factor contributing to the lack of socio-economic diversity in the professions. The share of employers that will accept applicants with *any* UCAS tariff, for example, has however risen by a further five percentage points in the last year (AGR, 2017).

However, unless this more inclusive approach to accepting candidates' applications is matched with a critical review of the tools used to select them, little progress will be made. Some graduate selection tools, especially those used in mass recruitment (e.g. traditional online numerical tests) intrinsically disadvantage candidates from lower socio-economic groups. It is so because they are less likely to be in a peer group undertaking the same tests, typically have less access to test coaching (e.g. from a careers service, or the employer visiting campus), and are more likely to withdraw from the process when scoring weakly in online practice tests (AGR, 2017).

More employers are introducing 'strengths-based assessment' in selection processes, which has been shown to deliver a focus on potential over previous experiences (up to 19% in 2016, compared to 7% in 2015) (AGR, 2017). This is in comparison to competency-based interviews, which typically include a series of enquiries at the interviewer's discretion, and require a candidate to draw on experiences that exemplify particular skills, which creates opportunities for bias.

There is increasing evidence regarding conscious bias in relation to recruitment practices, and the way in which some employers can mistake confidence and privilege for competence. Studies have found that definitions of talent within the professions are closely aligned with characteristics such as 'polish', confidence and certain forms of cultural competence; these aptitudes or competencies are arguably easier to acquire for individuals from more affluent backgrounds. In this context, recruiters may focus on proxies for quality such as social background and education, or 'appropriate' speech and mannerisms, in addition to apparently more objective measures such as credentials and qualifications (Ashley et al., 2015).

CLOSING REMARKS

Universities in the UK can only contribute meaningfully to increasing social mobility if the focus on widening participation is matched with an effort to narrow the gap in graduate outcomes by socio-economic background. This will require collective responsibility, and collaborative action, from across education sectors, government and employers. It will also require a more sophisticated understanding of the way in which diversity in education, and in the workplace, is to the advantage of all. This narrative should prevail over a deficit model, which diagnoses some students as lacking in certain attributes and, as a consequence, needing remedial intervention.

Additionally, the following three fundamental considerations must be included:

- the measurement of student success, building on (but not moving away from) graduate earnings;
- understanding diversity *within* the community of students from lower socio-economic backgrounds; and
- ensuring that in considering employers, we recognise that small and medium-sized enterprises account for 99.3% of private sector businesses in the UK.

The reward for this endeavour will be significant: a HE system that contributes significantly to improving socio-economic diversity amongst those with influence in our society and, thereby, a sector that can be authentically characterised as world leading.

REFERENCES

ACCA. (2015). Intern Aware and YouGov. Retrieved from https://yougov.co.uk/news/2011/03/23/investigating-internships/. Accessed on March 5, 2018.

AGCAS. (2013). *Graduate success project report*. London: AGCAS.

Ashley, L., Duberley, J., Sommerlad, H., Scholarios, D., & Social Mobility and Child Poverty Commission, Corp. Creator. (2015). *A qualitative evaluation of non-educational barriers to the elite professions*. London: Social Mobility Commission.

Association of Graduate Recruiters (AGR). (2016a). *Annual survey*. London: AGR.

Association of Graduate Recruiters (AGR). (2016b). *Diversity survey*. London: AGR.

Association of Graduate Recruiters (AGR). (2017). *Annual survey*. London: AGR.

Bradley, H., & Ingram, N. (2013). Banking on the future: Choices, aspirations and economic hardship in working-class student experience. In W. Atkinson, S. Roberts, & M. Savage (Eds.), *Class inequality in austerity Britain (p. 51)*. Basingstoke: Palgrave Macmillan.

Bridge Group (BG). (2016a). *Bridging the gaps: Student employability and progression*. London: BG.

Bridge Group (BG). (2016b). *Socio-economic diversity in the Fast Stream*. London: BG.

Bridge Group (BG). (2017a). *Interim rural and coastal working group report*. London: BG.

Bridge Group (BG). (2017b). *Social mobility and careers services*. London: BG.

Edelman Trust Barometer. (2017). Trust Barometer. Retrieved from www.edelman.co.uk/magazine/posts/edelman-trust-barometer-2017-uk-findings. Accessed on March 5, 2018.

Futuretrack. (2013). Learning from Futuretrack: The Impact of Work Experiences on Higher Education Student Outcomes. Retrieved from https://warwick.ac.uk/fac/soc/ier/futuretrack/news1/stage_4_report_final_06_03_2013.pdf. Accessed on March 5, 2018.

Higher Education Funding Council for England (HEFCE). (2016). *Differences in employment outcomes: Comparison of 2008–09 and 2010–11 first degree graduates*. London: HEFCE.

Hooley, T., Johnson, C., & Neary, S. (2016). *Professionalism in careers*. London: CDI.

Institute for Fiscal Studies (IFS). (2014). *Socio-economic differences in university outcomes in the UK: Drop-out, degree completion and degree class*. London: IFS.

Institute for Fiscal Studies (IFS). (2017). *How English domiciled graduate earnings vary with gender, institution attended, subject and socio-economic background*. London: IFS.

Laurison, D., & Friedman, S. (2015). *Introducing the class ceiling: Social mobility and Britain's elite occupations*. London: London School of Economic Publishing.

Office for Fair Access (OFFA). (2017). *Access agreements for 2018–19: Key statistics and analysis*. London: OFFA.

Social Mobility Commission (SMC). (2016). *State of the nation*. London: SMC.

Social Mobility Commission (SMC). (2017). *The Social Mobility Employer Index 2017*. Retrieved from http://www.socialmobility.org.uk/wp-content/uploads/2017/08/Social-Mobility-Employer-Index-2017-Key-findings.pdf. Accessed on March 5, 2018.

Trendence. (2018). Research. Retrieved from https://www.trendence.com/en/company/about-trendence.html. Accessed on March 5, 2018.

Universities UK. (2015). *Why Invest in Universities?* Retrieved from http://www.universitiesuk.ac.uk/policy-and-analysis/reports/Documents/2015/why-invest-in-universities.pdf. Accessed on March 5, 2018.

UK CES. (2016). *Working futures 2014–2024*. London: UK CES.

UK Higher Education International Unit. (2015). *Gone international: Mobile students and their outcomes*. Retrieved from http://europa.eu/rapid/press-release_IP-14-1025_en.htm. Accessed on March 5, 2018.

SECTION C

INNOVATIONS IN ACCESS TO SUCCESS

10

STUDENTS NOT PATIENTS: OPENING UP THE UNIVERSITY TO THOSE WITH MENTAL HEALTH PROBLEMS

Simon Newton and Nick Rowe

ABSTRACT

People with long-term experience of mental health problems can find it difficult to access higher education. The loss of confidence, social isolation and the stigma that often comes with mental ill health can make entering a university a daunting and intimidating experience. In this chapter, we consider Converge, a project which seeks to provide educational opportunities – across the campus of York St John University – to local people with mental health problems. The authors will suggest that the university environment and its people play a key role in supporting participants to learn, develop and progress. It is not medical or therapeutic interventions that make the difference, but learning within a socially valued and challenging environment.

Keywords: Mental health; widening participation; challenging stigma; learning communities; recovery; reciprocity

INTRODUCTION

'I stood outside the mental health centre watching students going to the university. I felt envious, wishing I could go but knowing that I never would'. Jane, Converge *participant*

A university can intimidate or welcome. It can define its quality through its exclusivity or through the distinctive value it can add to the student's knowledge. More recently, in response to the changing economic and social climate, universities are increasingly engaging with their local community, and developing strategies for supporting and focussing on students as socially aware citizens. Often described as civic engagement, universities demonstrate their social commitment through a wide range of approaches (Boland, 2014; Butin, 2010).

This chapter is about space and discusses how a university environment can play a part in social justice, challenging stigmatised identities and inviting a re-evaluation of self. Universities are valued by society. They carry messages about how we are to be appraised and how we are to behave. As these ivory towers open their doors, they provide opportunities to those who previously thought such hallowed spaces were out of reach. In this chapter, we consider the implication of this in the mental health field. If universities are institutions valued by society, psychiatric hospitals have traditionally carried very different implications. Even at the start of the twenty-first century, the psychiatric hospital is still redolent of a history of control and constraint. The stigma that surrounds our conceptions of 'madness', evoked by the old asylums, still haunts us.

Universities are very different spaces. They remain places of hope and aspiration, orientated towards the future. In our society, they are perhaps one of the places closest to the aspiration for recovery-focussed interventions in mental health. Rethink (2011) suggests the following four components of recovery: finding and maintaining hope; the re-establishment of positive identity; finding meaning in life and taking responsibility for one's life. Universities are places where such positive attributes are most likely to flourish. In this chapter, we will consider *Converge*, a project based at York St John University in the UK, which offers educational opportunities to local people with mental health problems.

The project can be seen as a model through which a university can build social capital, make a sustained contribution to the local community whilst simultaneously shaping a distinctive place in the higher education (HE) market place.

CONVERGE AND THE 'HEALING CAMPUS'

Converge is a project providing a wide range of educational opportunities to people with severe and often enduring mental health problems. It challenges the exclusivity that can surround HE and provides access for previously excluded groups.

This distinctive project is a partnership between York St John University and the local National Health Service Mental Health Trust. It delivers courses in music, theatre, dance, fine art, creative writing, design, psychology and sports exercise to people who use mental health services. All courses take place on campus and involve university students in delivery and support. The project also runs a choir with over 40 members and a theatre company, *Out of Character*, both comprising university students, staff and people who use local mental health services. In the academic year 2016–2017, *Converge* offered 37 courses; 318 people completed the courses and over 60 other university students were involved in delivery, support and research.

Key ingredients in the effectiveness of *Converge* are closely linked to those that lead to successful recovery including the generation of hope, social inclusion, overcoming isolation, engagement in supportive relationships, the strengthening of an enduring sense of self and the development of a sense of meaning and purpose (Ellison, Belanger, Niles, Leigh, & Bauer, 2018).

Therefore, the purpose of the *Converge* project is to challenge the dynamics of social exclusion which make it difficult for people who use mental health services to access good quality educational and employment opportunities. The second imperative is to provide opportunities to university students to learn through working alongside people who use mental health services. This can enhance students' employability through real-world experience and challenge stigmatising attitudes to mental illness. This is the *convergence* of core interests between a university and a mental health services provider from which the initiative takes its name.

It also aims to make the privileges and opportunities of HE accessible to people who are often marginalised from mainstream society. It seems to align with Butin's perspective, by aiming to bring about a situation, 'where the personal and the political meet in a substantive practice and where higher education is viewed as a central agent of change for an equitable society' (Butin 2010, p. 135).

WHO, WHERE AND WHAT: IDENTITY, PLACE AND ACTIVITY

The work of *Converge* is designed to challenge the stigma of mental illness. Link and Phelan (2010) set out the damaging consequences of stigma.

> *It begins when dominant groups distinguish human differences – whether real or not. It continues if the observed difference is believed to connote unfavourable information about the designated persons ... labelled persons are set apart in a distinct category that separates 'us' from 'them'. The differences lead to various forms of disapproval, rejection, exclusion and discrimination. (Link and Phelan cited in Rogers and Pilgrim 2010)*

One of the most corrosive effects of stigma is the way that it influences perception and expectation (Corrigan & Watson, 2002). For these reasons, in order to change the dynamics of powerlessness, it is important to engage people in activities, roles and places that are valued by society. For Wolfensberger (2000), this is the essential characteristic of what he called 'social role valorization'. This notion is central to the *Converge* model. In the following sections, we explore this approach in relation to identity, space, collaboration and support.

IDENTITY AND HEALING THE 'FRACTURE'

Questions of identity are central to the history and experience of people who have used mental health services (Link & Phelan, 2006). Therefore, *Converge* follows a twofold strategy. It frames the work as 'education not therapy' and works with people as students not patients or clients. Framing the activity as education begins from the first publicity about the activity, stressing learning rather than therapeutic benefit. It continues with the ways in which courses are organised and presented.

It is well established that the attribution of a mental health identity can lead to social isolation, a reduced sense of personal control, loss of hope and a focus on deficit rather than ability. At the heart of the *Converge* approach is the aim to work with people as students not 'patients' and deliver education not therapy. This simple reframing challenges the corrosive nature of the mental illness identity, which can reduce aspirations and inhibit recovery.

Obviously, it is good to witness clear signs of recovery; however, this is not often discussed. The model is a university one in which education is the aim and not therapy or direct health care. The *Converge* project invites and encourages participants to take as full a part in university life as possible. This enables the first steps towards recovery and 'developing a positive identity outside of being a person with a mental illness' (Slade, 2009, p. 83).

However, the separation of people with mental health problems from the community still needs addressing and the university can play its part in becoming what we are calling here, 'a healing campus' (Rowe, 2015). We might consider it an attempt to heal the 'fracture' between people who experience mental health problems and their communities that began with their disappearance into large mental hospitals in the eighteenth and nineteenth centuries – in what Michel Foucault (2001) called, 'the great confinement'. It was a fracture deepened by medicalisation and professional power – the scars of which still remain in the stigma that continues to surround mental ill health; and the lack of 'parity of esteem' between mental health and physical health care.

The benefits of the *Converge* model are reciprocal. The *Converge* strategic alliance[1] aims to:

(1) Offer good quality educational opportunities.

(2) Provide an opportunity for university students to work alongside people who use mental health services, enhancing their employability, and providing 'real world' experience and

(3) Challenge the dynamics of social exclusion that make it difficult for people who use mental health services to access good quality education.

In a reciprocal exchange, each should derive mutual benefit. This reciprocity is exemplified in the following:

• Students and staff share knowledge and skills of their subject area.

• People with mental health problems share their experience and knowledge.

• The whole university community learns to work alongside people with very different life experiences.

• Mental health service providers benefit from the different approaches and world views a university brings.

• A university campus asks for behaviours and attitudes (punctuality, tolerance, strict controls on drug and alcohol use in class) that can provide structure and clear boundaries for participants.

• *Converge* participants make use of many of the university's resources: they are associate members of the

---

1 A strategic convergence of interests between a university, its staff and students, *Converge* participants and mental health service providers.

students' union; have borrowing rights in the library; use the catering outlets; write, and publish a newsletter; teach short courses and mentor new project participants.

- Librarians support *Converge* students to use the IT services.

- Catering staff know many of the *Converge* students and welcome them when they enter.

- Our receptionists regularly come into contact with *Converge* students and treat them as students, whilst acknowledging the different needs they may have.

- A music student helps a *Converge* participant to arrange one of the songs he has written.

Such reciprocity is the key to a university becoming a healing campus or what Marullo and Edwards (2000) call 'an agent of social transformation'. They write:

> *University collaborative efforts afford us opportunities we cannot afford to miss: (a) helping to develop [student and staff] community service volunteers into social justice activists and (b) transforming institutions of higher education into agents of social transformation. (2000, p. 911)*

This reciprocity within a university environment illustrates what Chupp and Joseph (2010) call 'service learning with institutional change' (p. 197) that enriches the life of the university community and encourages attitudes that promote social justice.[2] It is a vision of what Marullo and Edwards (2000) called 'a transformed academy'.

---

2 See Chapter 11 by Wall, Giles, & Stanton in the present volume.

VALUED SPACES

When people are marginalised and often socially excluded, as is often the case with people who have mental health problems, activities should take place in spaces and institutions that are valued by society such as universities, mainstream theatres and properly appointed theatre spaces. Space contextualises an activity and gives it meaning. It shapes – and is shaped by – those who enter it. Space shapes expectation; in addition, to a considerable extent, it shapes roles. It is a crucial part of the project that activity takes place in a university. Universities are places of hope and optimism. To work with people in this environment invites a positive re-evaluation of selfhood.

WORKING TOGETHER: A COMMUNITY OF LEARNERS

To some extent, *Converge* echoes the values of the late Victorian Settlement movement when Samuel Barnett established a hostel in London's East End where a group of Oxford University students would share meals with the poor and offer educational courses to improve their circumstances. In 1884, Barnett urged students and staff at Oxford to 'bring the life of the university to bear on the life of the poor' (Scotland, 2007, p. 13). He was keen that students would be there 'to learn as much as to teach, to receive as much as to give' (Simkin, 2014). This sentiment of reciprocity is at the heart of the *Converge* model, echoing a phrase that is often used within the project: a 'community of learners' – a term that clearly resonates with that of 'learning communities' in which the learning is not so much about the acquisition of knowledge as about 'participation in a learning process' (Billingham, 2007, p. 26).

Just as advantaged groups spend most time with those in a similar position, disadvantaged groups can do the same. Education has the potential to bridge social divisions and develop contacts between usually divided social groups. In his key text, *The Nature of Prejudice* (1979), first published in 1954, Gordon Allport argues that, under certain conditions, interpersonal contact is one of the most effective ways to reduce prejudice between members of 'in-groups' and 'out-groups'. In their meta-analysis of the evidence of the 'contact hypothesis', Pettigrew and Tropp (2006) concluded that their results 'provide substantial evidence that intergroup contact can contribute meaningfully to reductions in prejudice across a broad range of groups and contacts' (p. 766). Not only do attitudes towards the immediate participants usually become more favourable, but also the attitudes towards the entire 'out group'; to 'out-group' members in other situations; and even 'out-groups' not involved in the contact.

SUPPORT

Some of the *Converge* participants need support to settle in to the university. Entering an unfamiliar environment, meeting new people and being engaged in new activities can be a daunting prospect. When people have had long histories of mental health problems or acute episodes that make them sensitive to stress and change, these difficulties can seem insurmountable. The stress of starting in HE for people who experience mental health problems is well documented (Jacklin, Robinson, O'Meara, & Harris, 2007). Support of new *Converge* participants is a role often taken by university students in the 'student buddy scheme' and *Converge* students in 'the peer mentor project'.

Through the 'buddy' scheme, university students (often, but not exclusively, training as health professionals) provide support to *Converge* students. This is best understood as student-to-student mentoring and such peer mentoring in HE has become increasingly common. Collins, Swanson, and Watkins (2014) found that peer-mentored individuals 'show higher levels of integration in the university' and such a support may 'buffer the effect of transition to university' (p. 927). In the 2016–2017 academic year, 32 university students provided support to over 60 Converge students.

Our peer-mentor project recognises the value of mutual support in mental health. This has always taken place informally. However, in the last few years, there has been a significant development in providing more formal peer-support arrangements. In their review of the literature on peer support in mental health, Repper and Carter (2011) stress that reciprocity is integral to the process of peer support, stating that:

> ...relationships that peers have with each other
> are valued for their reciprocity; they give an
> opportunity for sharing experiences, both giving
> and receiving support and for building up a mutual
> synergistic understanding that benefits both parties.
> (pp. 394–395)

However, there are risks that this contact will merely reinforce existing attitudes and power relations unless it is underpinned by critical understanding of the politics of mental health and by institutional change. In their critical overview of service learning, Chupp and Joseph (2010) proposed that projects, which involve students in community service as part of their educational experience should aim for impact at three levels: 'on students, on the academic institution and on the community' (p. 190). Only by working for impact across these groups can such ventures ensure social justice rather than merely offer charitable activities that tend to reinforce existing power relations.[3]

CONCLUSION

In *The Sociological Imagination* (1959), C. Wright Mills calls for a humanist sociology that connects the individual to the wider social, cultural and political forces that act on their lives and problems. The principles we have set out in this chapter are connected by an attempt to call upon the socio-logical imagination to address current issues in mental health practice. Personhood, social value and reciprocity envisages mental health practice as an act of social engagement within a nexus of interconnected influences and forces.

We want to conclude by drawing on a remarkable passage written about the Peckham Experiment – a health innovation that took place in the UK in the first half of the twentieth century:

> *Have you ever thought that health may be infectious? That it might spread through a community? That family after family could 'catch' it, and in catching it evolve a healthy society? [...] health grows and spreads, not by treatment of sickness, not by prevention of disease, not primarily through any form of correction, whether of physical or social ills, but through* cultivation of the social soil *[our emphasis]. (Pearse, 1943, p. i)*

---

3 See also Chapter 11 by Wall, Giles, & Stanton in the present volume.

Converge calls for a change from regarding people who use mental health services as ontologically different, highly vulnerable and in need of special care and treatment, to engage with them as students, artists, musicians or theatre makers. We suggest that this reframing of the mental health identity is enhanced and reinforced by the 'social soil' in which it takes place: a university campus.

REFERENCES

Allport, G. W. (1979). *The nature of prejudice*. Cambridge, MA: Perseus Books.

Billingham, S. (2007). Learning communities in tertiary education. In C. Clay, M. Madden, & L. Potts (Eds.), *Towards understanding community*. London: Palgrave MacMillan.

Boland, J. (2014). Orientations to civic engagement: Insights into the sustainability of a challenging pedagogy. *Studies in Higher Education*, *39*(1), 180–195.

Butin, D. (2010). *Service-learning in theory and practice. The future of community engagement in higher education*. New York, NY: Palgrave Macmillan.

Chupp, M., & Joseph, M. (2010). Getting the most out of service learning: Maximizing student, university and community impact. *Journal of Community Practice*, *18*, 190–212.

Collins, R., Swanson, V., & Watkins, R. (2014). The impact of peer mentoring on levels of student wellbeing, integration and retention: A controlled comparative evaluation of residential students in UK higher education. *Higher Education*, *68*(6), 927–942.

Corrigan, P., & Watson, A. (2002). Understanding the impact of stigma on people with mental illness. *World Psychiatry*, *1*(1) 16–20.

Ellison, N., Belanger, L., Niles, B., Leigh, C., & Bauer, M. (2018). Explication and definition of mental health recovery: A systematic review. *Administration and Policy in Mental Health and Mental Health Services Research*, *45*(1), 91–102.

Foucault, M. (2001). *Madness and civilization: A history of insanity in the age of reason*. (R. Howard, Trans.). London: Routledge.

Goffman, E. (1968). *Stigma: Notes on the management of spoiled identity*. London: Penguin.

Jacklin, A., Robinson, C., O'Meara, L., & Harris, A. (2007). *Improving the experiences of disabled students in higher education*. York: Higher Education Academy.

Lefebvre, H. (1991). *The production of space* (D. Nicholson-Smith, Trans.). Oxford: Blackwell.

Link, B. G., & Phelan, Jo. C. (2006). Stigma and its public health implications. *Lancet*, *367*, 528–529.

Marullo, S., & Edwards, B. (2000). From charity to justice: The potential of university-community collaboration for social change. *America Behavioral Scientist*, *43*(5), 895–912.

Massey, D. (2005). *For space*. London: Sage.

Pearse, I., & Crocker, L. (1943). *The Peckham experiment*. Sydney: George Allen and Unwin Ltd.

Pettigrew, T. F., & Tropp, L. R. (2006). A meta-analytic test of intergroup contact theory. *Journal of*

Personality and Social Psychology, 90(5), 751–783. doi: 10.1037/0022-3514.90.5.751

Repper, J., & Carter, T. (2011). A review of the literature on peer support in mental health services. *Journal of Mental Health, 20*(4), 392–411.

Rethink. (2011, August 11). Stigma and Mental Illness. Retrieved from http://www.rethink.org/living_with_men tal_illness/everyday_living/stigma_mental_illness/

Rowe, N. (2015). Creating a healing campus: A partnership between a university and a provider of mental health services. *University Partnerships for Community and School System Development, 5*, 119–134. Online: Emerald Insight.

Rowe, N., Forshaw, N., & Alldred, G. (2013). A return to ordinariness: How does working alongside people who use mental health services effect theatre students' attitudes to mental illness? *Journal of Applied Arts and Health, 4*(2), 151–162.

Scotland, N. (2007). *Squires in the slums: Settlements and missions in late Victorian Britain.* London: I. B. Tauris.

Simkin, J. (2014). Toynbee Hall. Retrieved from http:// spartacus-educational.com/EDtoynbeeH.htm. Accessed on May 26, 2015.

Wolfensberger, W. (2000, April). A brief overview of social role valorization. *Mental Retardation, 38*(2), 105–123.

Wright Mills, C. (1959). *The sociological imagination.* Oxford: Oxford University Press.

11

SERVICE LEARNING AND ACADEMIC ACTIVISM: A REVIEW, PROSPECTS AND A TIME FOR REVIVAL

Tony Wall, Dwight E. Giles, Jr and Tim Stanton

ABSTRACT

Service-learning (SL) is an educational movement with roots in academic activism fuelled by commitments to accessibility, social mobility, social justice, community engagement, sustainable development and learning. Reviewing the voices of the original US 'pioneers' and contemporary practitioners over the last 30 years, this chapter argues that (1) contemporary SL has been 'mainstreamed' in various ways and (2) such a re-conceptualisation seems to have re-formatted educational commitments in line with contemporary economic framings and circumstances of higher education (HE). However, it also argues that beyond overt compliance and resistance, it is possible for practitioners and HE more broadly to create responses and spaces where educational adaptation and transformation can emerge. To facilitate such responses, it is important to embrace the strong driving force of passion and emotion, which can drive and sustain change agents in practice. This chapter aspires to revitalise and rejuvenate academic activism as a legitimate catalyst of educational transformation on a global platform.

Keywords: Experiential education; service learning; social justice; academic activism; pedagogical passion; transformational learning

INTRODUCTION: A DISRUPTIVE AND REBELLIOUS HISTORY

The first concrete expressions of service learning (SL) can be traced back to the 1950s and 1960s in the southeast USA, and specifically and surprisingly to the Oak Ridge Institute of Nuclear Studies in Tennessee (Stanton, Giles, & Cruz, 1999). However, its conceptual antecedents can be found in (1) the philosophy and practice of 'extension education' programmes spawned by the Land Grant university movement of the 1860s, (2) the 'progressive education' and urban settlement house activities in the last century, (3) work programmes of President Franklin Roosevelt's New Deal and (4) 1920s' immigrant education and 1960s' civil rights organising (Pollack, 1997). Indeed Stanton's great uncle, John Collier, engaged in activities in a lower Manhattan settlement house in the 1920s that very closely resembled his SL teaching. Therefore, social change was at the heart of SL.

With a panel of nominators, Stanton et al. (1999) identified 31 'founders' of the field; those who had up to that time the most influence on the field's development, whose influence came through advocacy, publications, or other means, as well as through example, or practice. They represented the most influential strands of SL history (e.g. experiential education and voluntary student action). These 'pioneers' traced their early motivations to take up this work to political events or issues taking place when they were young, including civil rights, anti-Vietnam war movements, resistance to the military draft and rural and urban poverty. The pioneers described their work in a variety of ways:

> *I saw my work as **an extension of the social movement of the 1960s**, and saw myself aligning with poor people's groups and organizing, being at least one avenue between these groups and movements or resources of more affluent communities. My motivation was **political change**. Michelle Whitham. (Stanton et al., 1999, p. 75)*

> *I thought of my work not as a job but as working from a base for moving a movement forward within higher education … **a movement for social change in the wider world**. Nadinne Cruz (Stanton et al., 1999, p. 75)*

> *You have to show them [students] how you can use sociology to understand something about the world and **use that as a template for altering it** … Jon Wagner. (Stanton et al., 1999, p. 63)*

> *I … stood at the edge of the university, so I could hand out some machinery that the university wasn't using and find places for students to get out of the*

> *curriculum that they didn't find satisfying and get into learning experiences that they did. I saw myself as an **educator … and an agent of change, trying to push the boundaries of the institution further towards the community**. Dick Couto. (Stanton et al., 1999, p. 81)*

The pioneers tended to view pedagogy, which combined community action with critical reflection, as a means of addressing them in an educational context. Some were more focused on educational questions; others on issues of social justice and still others were most interested in preparing students for effective, democratic engagement. All of them were deeply concerned with educational and social change, echoing the sentiments and practices of others in this book.

Thus, these early days of working in SL were dangerous. A great majority of these pioneers had their programmes shut down or their jobs terminated, or both, because they 'did' SL. They described their professional lives as marginal, often lonely and embattled. They might have been the only staff person on their campus committed to this work, which was not understood or respected by most academic staff and administrators, and for which they had to scramble for institutional support and survival. The institutional challenges were formidable. The pioneers had great difficulty sustaining their programmes, attributing the difficulties they encountered to trying to promote:

- teaching in research-oriented institutions;

- interdisciplinary study in discipline-controlled settings;

- 'suspect', experiential pedagogy in a culture that valued traditional, hierarchical knowledge concepts (trying to 'replace Plato with Dewey');

- learning off-campus, which could not be 'controlled' by faculty; and

- education for social justice in a culture, which viewed education as value-neutral.

Lacking both status and influence, these pioneers were under continuous attack just to maintain their institutional base. Indeed, almost all the pioneers were ousted, had their programmes shut down or resigned from a SL position at one point of time in their career.

MARGINS TO MAINSTREAM – WHO BENEFITS?

By the mid-1990s, some SL advocates, still frustrated with the slow acceptance of SL pedagogy within the academic mainstream, began to ask whether SL had a future (Zlotkowski, 1995). They called for a concerted effort to institutionalise the work through connecting service and study, especially by engaging more traditional faculty colleagues and building SL into the disciplines. The American Association for Higher Education published, over a 10-year period (1997–2006), a widely circulated series of books, many of which examined SL's applications.

Combined with increasing research showing that SL generated valid learning, it seemed that SL was being legitimised in the mainstream (Eyler & Giles, 1999; Giles, 2010; Giles & Eyler, 2013; Giles, Honnet, & Migliore, 1991). Indeed, the 1991 Wingspread Conference was established to develop a research agenda for combining service and learning. At that point, the Conference raised a number of issues:

> *When [my Chancellor] wanted to start a program*
> *and send students into these communities where*

they would learn, I stood against him. We would have huge debates. I was in favor of students serving, but when he said students will go down there, study the community, write essays [where] students will learn, I said **what does the community get out of it?** *... If we left it [service-learning] in the control of the universities and students,* **they would use the communities to their service, to their own benefit, and not think about what happens.** *Herman Blake (Stanton et al., 1999, p. 128)*

If we are going to stay organized as a department of economics, department of social sciences and departments of this that and the other, and that's the way we are sending our students out from those departmental, narrow gauge perspectives and disciplines, **we are going to do damage to communities and to students in the way they are thinking.** *Robert Sigmon (Stanton et al.., p. 225)*

However, critics of this and other 'adaptive' strategies to embed SL within the academic structures began asking whether a consequence of doing so would de-emphasise SL's interdisciplinary, transformative potential (Stanton, 1998). More recently, a drift away from SL's original community impact and social justice concerns has been identified (Pollack, 2015; Sheffield, 2015); perhaps, caused in part by the emphasis to embed this pedagogy within the curriculum. For example, Pollack (1997) locates this drift in SL concepts articulated over four decades of related Federal legislation; from its first appearance in the *Domestic Volunteer Service Act* (PL 93–113) in 1973 (United States Congress, 1973) where its purpose was,

to strengthen and supplement efforts to eliminate poverty and poverty-related human social and

> environmental problems" ... to the **National Service**
> **Act** of 1990 where it has been transformed from an
> anti-poverty program to an educational "method ...
> to enhance what is taught in school" (p. 165) ...
> Taken together, the impact of these forces has resulted
> in a twisted, appropriated institutionalization process,
> the cultural reworking of an epistemologically
> transformative educational practice into a teaching
> method. (Pollack, 2015, p. 167)

In the last decade, many institutions have chosen to reframe their SL as 'civic' or 'community engagement' (Saltmarsh, 2005; Saltmarsh & Hartley, 2011). These terms provide a broader umbrella for experiential learning in the community through volunteerism, research, advocacy and other means with SL being one strand. For example, Stanford University's Haas Center for Public Service has articulated 'Pathways to Public Service' as central to its mission, which include activism, community-engaged scholarship, direct service, philanthropy, policy/politics and social entrepreneurship (Hass Center for Public Service, 2015).

Critics of this new terminology and broader umbrella ask whether they refocus SL too much on student development with a consequential erosion of commitment to collaborative, community-responsive action with community partners. A similar trend has emerged in relation to the reconceptualisation of SL (and experiential or work-based learning) for employability outcomes (Wall & Perrin, 2015). At the SL Gathering held in Golden Colorado in May 2017, SL practitioners echoed these concerns. For example, one practitioner crossing various academic and practitioner boundaries said:

> My definition has changed over time. I entered the
> work through the door of service-learning and very

*much identify with the service-learning field. Over
time the work that I do has changed. Right now
… I am Assistant Vice-Chancellor for Community
Engagement. The term feels good to me in the
sense that it encompasses the community-campus
partnership work that I do. But it also is problematic
… I have come across many, many circumstances
where I have become concerned by the lack of
principles and purposes that animate the work.…
The concern for me is the growth in the field …
how do we retain quality? … The people … who …
started this work were intimately motivated to have
the highest qualities of experiences and saw their
opportunity to do this work as transformational.…
As we've grown I don't know if that's true for
everyone at this moment …* **close personal concern
for the high quality of relationship development is
not always embedded in the work.** *Lina Dostilio
(personal communication, 18 May, 2017)*

A REVIVAL OF PROVOCATION AND DISRUPTION

Although some have described the mainstreaming of SL as
'a retreat' from its roots, the role of the individual SL 'zealot'
still seems to be crucial in establishing and sustaining SL commitments (Bennett, Sunderland, Bartleet, & Power, 2016). The
role of the individual to act as an academic activist, in order
to lead and challenge existing pedagogical infrastructures and
systems, seems to be as important now as it was 30 years ago.
Yet, it may well be even more important in contemporary circumstances given the naturalised way in which the economic
framings of higher education (HE) are accepted (Wall, 2017b;
Wall & Jarvis, 2015; Wall & Perrin, 2015).

Within this context, it is important to acknowledge that particular moral values towards making a difference in communities have an important role in driving through SL efforts, even with the prospects of potential negative impacts on tenureship (Cooper, 2014). This highlights and foregrounds the important role of morals and emotional responses in directing meaningful action, and indeed, their role in sense making in the context of SL (Larsen, 2017). In sensing the need to respond to contemporary circumstances, such moral and emotional responses will direct individuals, who lead SL efforts, to align to one of three potential responses (Taylor, 2017).

The first is *compliance*, where the status quo is valued and lived out by the practitioner – thus, not the genuine realm for an academic activist. The second is *resistance*, where the practitioner openly retaliates against the system to propose alternatives. This can be a high-risk strategy for an activist, as it can amplify binary options which are then labelled in ways which emphasise the importance of the status quo (Wall, 2016a, 2016c; Wall et al., 2017a). A third response calls for the crafting of *hybrid approaches,* which seem to integrate potentially conflicting agendas; for example, conceptualising SL not just within the context of employability or just within the context of community development (Taylor, 2017).

New directions might creatively combine agendas, which speak to sustainable development and change-agency capacities within diverse communities (Alden Rivers, Armellini, & Nie, 2015; Rivers, Armellini, Maxwell, Allen, & Durkin, 2015; Wall, 2016b, 2017a, 2017b; Wall et al., 2017a, 2017b). This calls for the ingenuity of academic activists to re-conceptualise their work in ways, which speak to the roots of SL, thus simultaneously (1) challenging those infrastructures and systems, by (2) re-packaging programmes and activities in ways, which *navigate* infrastructures and systems.

Paradoxically, this typically involves knowing the intimate details of the infrastructures and systems, knowing the inherent logics and justifications and then *utilising* them to justify and enact the proposed innovations (Bennett et al., 2016).

The response that is chosen (or enacted) will provide the parameters as to the potentially disruptive nature of SL efforts. As contemporary forms of education have been critiqued for maintaining the status quo (or even 'damaging the community' – see earlier discussion), it is important to rejuvenate the more radical provocative and disruptive nature of SL (Sheffield, 2015). This includes dealing with forms of SL, which engage over longer periods, and moving beyond Dewey's 'felt difficulties' towards 'difficult knowledge' (Sheffield, 2015). Such forms of knowledge do not have simple answers or any immediate resolution as such (e.g. institutional racism), but engage a wider range of capacities and resources.

Academic activists who move in such ways resonate with a broader family of provocative forms of educational activity, which promote forms of learning less characterised by individual outcomes, reflections and satisfaction, and more by collective outcomes and impacts and potentially dissatisfaction with the status quo (Wall, 2016a, 2016b, 2016c, 2017b; Wall & Jarvis, 2015; Wall et al., 2017a). Again, this is echoed in the other chapters of this book, such as Rowe and Newton's reflective description of Converge, where roles become creatively disrupted: This belongs to a family of such educational approaches which is much more interested in the facilitation of insights and changes in practice than learning pre-set answers or even pre-set formulae – a family much more oriented towards the roots of SL conceptualised over three decades ago.

In this way, being an academic activist in contemporary education is about re-centring the human, humane and emotional aspects of learning in practice; to propel us to act and make a difference in the context of real life. Although this is the stuff of academic activism, it seems there is some difficult knowledge about the HE system we need to develop. As one practitioner at The National Service – Learning Gathering of 2017 says:

> *What does keep me up at night if I am thinking… is this idea of connecting our emotions to empathy and the way in which that is not allowed in the academy. That may be the next dimension to open up. Emily Janke (personal communication; 18 May, 2017)*

REFERENCES

Alden Rivers, B., Armellini, A., & Nie, M. (2015). Embedding social innovation and social impact across the disciplines: Identifying 'changemaker' attributes. *Higher Education, Skills and Work-Based Learning*, 5(3), 242–257.

Bennett, D., Sunderland, N., Bartleet, B., & Power, A. (2016). Implementing and sustaining higher education service-learning initiatives: Revisiting Young et al.'s organizational tactics. *Journal of Experiential Education*, 39(2), 145–163.

Cooper, J. R. (2014). Ten years in the trenches: Faculty perspectives on sustaining service-learning. *Journal of Experiential Education*, 37(4), 415–428.

Eyler, J., & Giles, D. E. (2010). *Where is the learning in service-learning?* San Francisco, CA: Jossey-Bass.

Giles, D. E. (2010). Journey to service-learning research: Agendas, accomplishments, & aspirations. In J. Keshen & B. Moely (Eds.), *Advances in service learning research* (Vol. 10). Charlotte, NC: Information Age Press.

Giles, D. E., & Eyler, J. S. (2013). Review essay: "The endless quest for scholarly respectability in service-learning research". *Michigan Journal of Community Service Learning*, 20(1), 53–64.

Giles, D. E., Honnet, E. P., & Migliore, S. (Eds.). (1991). *Setting the agenda for effective research in combining service and learning in the 1990s*. Raleigh, NC: The National Society for Internships and Experiential Education.

Hass Center for Public Service. (2015). Pathways to public service. Retrieved from https://haas.stanford.edu/about/about-our-work/pathways-public-service. Accessed October 30, 2017.

Larsen, M. A. (2017). International service-learning: Rethinking the role of emotions. *Journal of Experiential Education*, 40(3), 279–294.

Pollack, S. S. (1997). *Three decades of service-learning in higher education (1966–1996): The contested emergence of an organizational field*. Unpublished Ph.D. thesis, Stanford University, Stanford.

Pollack, S. S. (2015). Critical civic literacy as an essential component of the undergraduate curriculum. In W. J. Jacob, S. E. Sutin, J. C. Weidman, & J. L. Yeager (Eds.), *Community engagement in higher education* (pp. 161–184). Pittsburgh Studies in Comparative and International Education. Rotterdam: Sense Publishers.

Rivers, B. A., Armellini, A., Maxwell, R., Allen, S., & Durkin, C. (2015). Social innovation education: Towards a framework for learning design. *Higher Education, Skills and Work-Based Learning*, 5(4), 383–400.

Saltmarsh, J. (2005). The civic promise of service learning. *Liberal Education*, 91(2), 50–55.

Saltmarsh, J., & Hartley, M. (Eds.). (2011). *"To serve a larger purpose": Engagement for democracy and the transformation of higher education*. Pennsylvania, PA: Temple University Press.

Sheffield, E. C. (2015). Toward radicalizing community service learning. *Educational Studies*, *51*(1), 45–56.

Stanton, T. (1998). Institutionalizing service-learning within postsecondary education: Transformation or social adaptation? *Partnership Perspectives*, *1*(1), 9–18.

Stanton, T. K., Giles, D. E., & Cruz, N. I. (1999). *Service learning: A movement's pioneers reflect on its origins, practice and future*. San Francisco, CA: Jossey-Bass.

Taylor, A. (2017). Service-learning programs and the knowledge economy: Exploring the tensions. *Vocations and Learning*, *10*(3), 253–273.

United States Congress. (1973). Domestic Volunteer Service Act. Public Law 93–113, 93rd Congress. Retrieved from https://www.nationalservice.gov/sites/default/files/documents/1973_domesticvolunteer_service_act_amendedthroughpl111_13.pdf.

Wall, T. (2016a). Author response: Provocative education: From the Dalai Lama's Cat® to Dismal Land®. *Studies in Philosophy and Education*, *35*(6), 649–653.

Wall, T. (2016b). Reviving the ubuntu spirit in landscapes of practice: Evidence from deep within the forest. *Journal of Work-Applied Management*, *8*(1), 95–98.

Wall, T. (2016c). Žižekian ideas in critical reflection: The tricks and traps of mobilising radical management insight. *Journal of Work-Applied Management*, *8*(1), 5–16.

Wall, T. (2017a). Reciprocal pedagogies: Flexible learning exemplar. In S. Devitt-Jones (Ed.), *Flexible learning practice guide* (pp. 20–23). York: HEA/QAA.

Wall, T. (2017b). A manifesto for higher education, skills and work-based learning: Through the lens of the manifesto for work. *Higher Education, Skills and Work-Based Learning*, 7(3), 304–314.

Wall, T., Hindley, A., Hunt, T., Peach, J., Preston, M., Hartley, C., & Fairbank, A. (2017a). Work-based learning as a catalyst for sustainability: A review and prospects. *Higher Education, Skills and Work-Based Learning*, 7(2), 211–224.

Wall, T., & Jarvis, M. (2015). *Business schools as educational provocateurs of productivity via interrelated landscapes of practice*. London: Chartered Association of Business Schools.

Wall, T., & Perrin, D. (2015). *Slavoj žižek: A žižekian gaze at education*. London: Springer.

Wall, T., Tran, L. T., & Soejatminah, S. (2017b). Inequalities and agencies in workplace learning experiences: International student perspectives. *Vocations and Learning*, 10(2), 141–156.

Zlotkowski, E. (1995). Does service-learning have a future? *Michigan Journal of Community Service Learning*, 20(2), 123–133.

12

WARMING A HIGHER EDUCATION COLD SPOT: THE CASE OF COVENTRY UNIVERSITY IN SCARBOROUGH

Craig Gaskell and Ian Dunn

ABSTRACT

This chapter outlines the development of 'CU Scarborough', a new campus of Coventry University Group, developed on the North Yorkshire coast in the UK. It is positioned as though it were a 'micro university' in and for an area of traditionally low participation in higher education – a so-called 'higher education cold spot'. This chapter provides an overview of the project highlighting: the motivation for the development; summarising the innovative academic model being applied; tracking the rapid journey from initial concept

*to the first students preparing to graduate and reflecting
on the impact being made to date.*

Keywords: Micro-university; university group; partnership;
social mobility; cold spot; academic enterprise

INTRODUCTION: THE SCARBOROUGH CONTEXT

The Yorkshire coastal strip has for some time been recognised as a cold spot[1] for higher education with only 23.3% of
people with a level 4 qualification or above, compared with
34.4% nationally (NOMIS, 2011). The Yorkshire Coast also
has the lowest mean employee gross salary of any part of the
UK (Corfe, 2017) and is highlighted as an area of low social
mobility, ranking 312 out of 324 districts in the government's
social mobility index (Social Mobility and Child Poverty
Commission and Social Mobility Commission, 2016). In an
attempt to improve social mobility, the area has been desig-
nated an Opportunity Area by the Department for Education
(2017).

The University of Hull operated a higher education (HE)
campus in Scarborough for 15 years. Hull adopted various
models for the campus with one approach yielding a period of
significant growth. In 2014, Hull took the decision to rationalise its provision onto a single campus in the city of Hull.
Following a managed withdrawal from the Scarborough site,
all undergraduate and postgraduate operations had ceased by
summer 2017 and the campus was sold to a regional Further
Education (FE) College group.

---

1 A HE cold spot is an area where there has been significantly lower participation in HE than the national average.

Scarborough Borough Council (SBC) and a number of their key strategic partners became very concerned about the potential economic and societal consequences of losing their HE campus. They investigated the possibility of developing their own university in Scarborough to support the Yorkshire coast, its rural hinterland and wider North Yorkshire. However, SBC formed a close working relationship with Coventry University Group, which led eventually to Coventry University announcing plans to develop a new campus in Scarborough in 2015.

The aim was to work closely with partners and businesses in the public and private sectors to develop provision aligned to the higher-level skills most needed in the region. The approach was to develop a new 'institution' in and for the region, with significant autonomy enabling alignment to its local context. However, the campus would be part of and fully supported by the wider Coventry University Group, adopting an innovative model of student focussed, accessible, career-oriented higher education that had been developed previously in Coventry.

AN ACADEMIC MODEL FOR SOCIAL INCLUSION

Coventry University College (CUC) was created in Coventry in 2011, as part of Coventry University Group in response to the increase in tuition fees that followed the Browne Review (Browne, 2010). It was anticipated that tuition fee changes were most likely to impact negatively on the most disadvantaged potential students; those from the lowest socio-economic groups, including students most likely to need to live at home. Accessibility, flexibility and removal of barriers to entry to high-quality higher education were primary drivers.

From the outset, successful progression into meaningful graduate careers was another key performance measure for

CUC. The fees were set low relative to sector norms. Access and Foundation programmes were provided for those who didn't fully meet the entry criteria for degree-level study. To mark a clear divide between the established academic offer already operating within the Faculties at Coventry University, and provide an enabling construct within which to develop a new higher education model from first principles, a wholly owned subsidiary of Coventry University, CUC Ltd., was created.

Fundamental to the new academic model is a block structure. Students study one module at a time in self-contained six-week blocks, which encapsulate *all* formal learning and assessment. Students need to complete four blocks at each stage of study, with each stage leading to a potential exit award. Exit on completion of the first stage (level 4) yields a Higher National Certificate; exit after stage 2 (level 5) yields a Higher National Diploma and completion of the final stage (level 6) yields an Honours Degree. Students can build up to a degree, stage by stage, with the possibility of breaks in between.

Academic progression occurs each time students move up a level. However, at a given stage, there is no prescribed sequence in which modules need to be taken. Modules are academically independent from each other but together they form the pre-requisites for the following stage. Full-time students complete four blocks each year with those starting in September finished by mid-April. By offering repeats of modules 1 and 2 in the summer, multiple (up to six) entry points are possible within any year.

Each module is built around the benchmark standards and Quality Assurance Agency norms and includes direct engagement with professional body standards and awards, where appropriate. In some cases, this means professional body recognition can be gained alongside academic awards to enhance student employability.

There are no optional modules and each module is organised around the principle of 20 hours of tuition each week. Classes take place either in the morning or the afternoon, over a contiguous period, each weekday. Students are either taught in the morning period or the afternoon period and this remains stable throughout their studies enabling students to work, or fit other responsibilities, around their studies.

APPLYING THE MODEL: A MICRO UNIVERSITY

The academic model developed for CUC was to form the basis of the new campus in Scarborough. However, the context for its application was very different. CUC had been developed in Coventry, the home city of Coventry University Group, in a building on the well-established University campus. Although CUC developed its own operations, these were embedded physically in the heart of the University's established infrastructure. The Coventry University brand was also well established and very strong in the area. The access agenda associated with CUC enabled students attracted to, but not accepted by, the existing university faculties to be offered a Foundation Route at CUC, facilitating rapid student population growth.

The Scarborough Campus, on the other hand, was established some 165 miles away from Coventry, a 4.5-hour train journey, in a different region. Very few students had been attracted to Coventry previously from the Yorkshire coast, and wider northern region more generally, and Coventry University had no supporting infrastructure in this area. The pull-factors were very strong from the supporting partners. However, to some outside the project, the idea of Coventry University Group coming to Scarborough was initially a bemusing concept.

Many universities around the world have operated branch or satellite campuses with a range of different strategies and trajectories evident. However, established faculty structures often transcend the different sites. This can create a constraining dynamic for development of the sites themselves as semi-autonomous entities suited to their local contexts (Gaskell & Hayton, 2014). In recent times, several universities in the UK have looked to rationalise their satellite sites to concentrate focus and investment at their main, often city-based, campus. The established UK university sector is facing major challenges with financial pressures and demographic changes. Smaller universities are under particular pressure (Gaskell, 2017).

HE can be, and often is, delivered in FE Colleges (so-called 'HE in FE'). In some cases, separate university centres have been established in FE colleges where delivery is at scale. However, the dominant business of these organisations is FE, which is generally poorly funded, and that can create a dynamic where the HE component of the operation subsidises the FE business.

As universities with satellite sites look to rationalise, and private providers remain cautious to invest in areas of low population density, there is a risk that significant parts of the population, particularly those living in areas remote from major urban centres, could become (or remain) cut off from accessing high quality HE. If students aren't able to 'go away' to university, there is a danger that areas of low social mobility will continue to persist, or even deteriorate.

The challenge in Scarborough was to create an institution that operated locally, as though it were a 'micro university', fully embedded in its region, fit for its local context, and with a strong set of local partnerships. At the same time, it was to be fully integrated into the parent organisation to leverage the power, expertise and investment capacity of a large, internationally focussed and entrepreneurial University Group.

Coventry University Scarborough Campus was developed as a sibling of CUC, within the same academic subsidiary. This enabled the academic model and regulatory infrastructure, developed previously for CUC, to be adopted in Scarborough. However, because CUC itself was young and its context was very different, the Scarborough campus also needed direct connection with and support from the wider University Group. There was a need to enable and empower the local team with significant autonomy to facilitate the necessary innovation. Learning also needed to be a two-way process because the Scarborough venture was breaking new ground for the wider Group.

FROM CONCEPT TO CAMPUS

The first member of Scarborough-based staff, the Founding Provost, had significant regional knowledge and was appointed in March 2015. From this point, design of the new campus building could be progressed at pace along with planning permission preparation works; development of the staffing model; preparation for academic delivery; local profile raising and progression of the partnership development activities. There was also important internal work to ensure the University Group understood, and could support, the Scarborough project.

In September 2015, 'Coventry University Scarborough Campus' was launched with a small freshly appointed start-up staff team and academic delivery commenced. Three degrees and an Access course were inherited from CUC. As no campus existed at this point, identification of temporary premises was needed. The Scarborough Spa, a conference and entertainment venue on the sea front was chosen as the primary delivery location; with a staff base and temporary library and learning resources centre established nearby.

Starting operations rapidly, all be it on a very small scale in September 2015, was important to provide a strong, stabilising, public signal locally, amid concerns around the loss of existing university provision. Starting small also enabled the assumptions around the portability of the academic model and operating concepts to be tested with a small '*pioneer*' student cohort.

In addition to commencing delivery, designing the new campus building, developing the staffing model and general profile raising, significant attention was given to building partnerships with key potential employers of students. Work also commenced to start development of the academic portfolio; understanding in detail the demands of the area and in some cases starting work with partners on degree programme co-design.

The new university building was commissioned in August 2016. This enabled the first intake of students onto the new campus in September that year. At this point, the campus was also re-branded as 'CU Scarborough', with the sibling operation in Coventry (CUC) re-branded, 'CU Coventry'.

The development site also included a new school and an extensive new Leisure Village. By May 2017, the new integrated £50 million Education and Sports Campus was complete with CU Scarborough at its heart. From September 2017, CU Scarborough students had a full campus experience available to them, with access to an onsite swimming pool, gym, fitness suite, sports hall, 4G football pitch and multiuse games area.

PROGRESS SO FAR

CU Scarborough moved into its third academic year of operation in September 2017 with the student population growing to 400 approximately. The majority of CU Scarborough activity is at levels 4, 5 and 6. Although there is a Sixth Form College locally, the general FE offer in the region is limited at level 3. Hence, provision of an Access to HE programme became important. Access cohorts have grown year on year with approximately 60 Access students on campus in 2017/18. Progression from Access to degree-level study has been strong. Students who have some level 3 qualifications, but not yet enough evidence to be accepted directly onto a degree course, can be registered for the Higher National Certificate (HNC) year only (the level 4 qualification). For some, this could be taken as a sub-degree exit award, providing enhanced career prospects and the opportunity to return for higher-level study at a later date. For others, successful completion of level 4 enables immediate progression onto the remaining two years of the Honours degree.

Despite the overt widening participation approach, the average *total* entry tariff for students joining CU Scarborough in 2016 and 2017 was above the equivalent of ABB at A-level (or Distinction-Distinction-Merit at BTEC Level 3 Extended Diploma). CU Scarborough is driving a widening access agenda, whilst at the same time attracting some students who, in pure entry tariff terms, would be accepted by some of the UK's most selective universities.

The age profile of students at CU Scarborough is higher than the sector norm with only 24% of undergraduate students aged 18 at the point of enrolment. 19.3% of the 2017 intake were aged 30 or above compared with a national figure of only 5.8% (HESA, 2018). The mean age of students across the CU Scarborough population as a whole is currently 28. Also, at the start of January 2018, 18% of CU Scarborough students had a known disability. This is well above the sector average of 12.5% (HESA, 2018).

As a cold spot, the Yorkshire coastal strip has historical low participation in HE. The creation of CU Scarborough is likely to start to show impact on these figures quickly. 61% of the intake in September 2017 came from Scarborough Borough itself (i.e., the North Yorkshire coast). Looking inland, a further 13% came from the City of York and surrounding hinterland. The remaining 26% were from a catchment outside the wider region, with 11% from outside Yorkshire and Humber entirely.

To date, the vast majority of students have come from the cold spot area itself with over 19% of entrants in September 2017 coming from so-called *low-participation neighbourhoods*. This compares to 12% for the HE sector as a whole (HESA, 2018).

A degree apprenticeship[2] offer has been launched, working with the developing employer partnership network. Apprenticeship students are on campus one day a week and are in full-time work for the rest of the time. The cohorts are 'open' enabling clusters of students from various different organisations to come together, providing the added advantage of inter-organisational networking and experience sharing (see also May & Jones in this volume, Chapter 6). Many are also commuting significant distances across the rural county for their study day. Through this delivery model, a more general 'one day a week on campus' or day-release study mode is developing.

The initial academic portfolio for CU Scarborough was formed by transferring a subset of established academic products from Coventry. Although this enabled a rapid launch, the portfolio wasn't ideal for the Scarborough context. Hence, a range of new academic programmes has been developed to enable better alignment to demand and take advantage of the local environment. In September 2017, six new degree programmes were launched, developed in close consultation – and

---

2 Degree apprenticeships enable students in full-time work to study for a degree at the same time.

in several cases developed via a co-design process – with local and regional partners.

Early engagement work highlighted that there was a significant challenge for the local NHS in attracting and retaining well-qualified nursing staff. Close collaboration between CU Scarborough, Coventry University's Faculty of Health and Life Sciences and the York and North Yorkshire NHS trust has enabled a BSc in Adult Nursing to be approved for delivery at CU Scarborough from 2018. This augments a range of provision offered in the Health Care domain – an area of significant local need and an area where university provision can make a major impact. There are a number of other developments working closely with local partners, which will produce additional academic provision over the next few years. However, the portfolio is now beginning to stabilise.

The new campus building has become established as a key venue for events, training, mini-conferences and wider business networking:

- A popular business breakfast series has been established with high-profile speakers, and over 50 businesses regularly in attendance.

- Local careers networks meet on site.

- A number of community-focussed projects and events are also hosted, with the campus used as a venue on the Scarborough festivals circuit.

- Regular 'stay-and-play' sessions for local toddlers take place, which also provide valuable practice experience for CU Scarborough's Early Childhood students.

- The campus is often used by local schools for aspiration raising events, helping children to become familiar and comfortable with a university environment from an early age.

- The building is also used by groups such as regional healthcare professionals and North Yorkshire Police for their own staff development events.

FINAL REFLECTIONS

Although in its infancy, CU Scarborough is already being embraced as a locally and regionally engaged institution, referred to in the area as 'the University'. At the same time, it leverages the advantages of being part of a wider, international, University Group. The relatively low population density and issues of low educational attainment and aspiration on the Yorkshire coast make CU Scarborough a challenging enterprise to develop. It is going against the tide of campus rationalisations evident in much of the UK HE sector. However, the opportunity to facilitate tangible and positive change for individuals, local communities, businesses, the public sector and the wider economy are clear; and the approach to develop a micro-university in this context is motivating a great deal of creativity and innovation.

Although a sibling, CU Scarborough has significant differences to CU Coventry. However, it has demonstrated that the same fundamental academic model, and same core principles can be applied successfully in very different contexts, with learning and experience able to be shared.

CU Scarborough has demonstrated that widening participation takes many forms. The traditionally held view that widening participation students are those from more socially deprived backgrounds or less academically advantaged areas is far too narrow. Clearly, it encompasses those aspects; however, improved social mobility and increased access to success can also be through the physical provision of higher education in an area where it is currently lacking; it is over an hour of travel time in any direction from Scarborough town to an established university.

The CU Scarborough venture is about the provision of high-quality choice, daring to be different, to enable a rich educational and social mix of students and staff. It is about working in genuine partnership with local partners, providing the conditions for learning from many perspectives.

ACKNOWLEDGEMENT

We are grateful to Gareth Smith for his data analysis work.

REFERENCES

Browne, J. (2010). Securing a sustainable future for higher education. An independent review of higher education funding and student finance. Retrieved from http://www.gov.uk/government/publications/the-browne-report-higher-education-funding-and-student-finance. Accessed on March 1, 2018.

Corfe, S. (2017). Living on the edge: Britain's coastal communities. The Social Market Foundation. Retrieved from http://www.smf.co.uk/wp-content/uploads/2017/09/Living-on-the-edge.pdf. Accessed on November 3, 2017.

Department for Education. (2017). North Yorkshire Coast Opportunity Area 2017-20: A Delivery Plan to Drive Social Mobility on the North Yorkshire Coast. Retrieved from https://www.gov.uk/government/uploads/system/uploads/attachment_data/file/654841/Social_Mobility_Delivery_Plan_NYC_v6.pdf. Accessed on March 1, 2018.

Gaskell, C. (2017). Leading small scale, new and evolving higher education institutions in turbulent times. SRHE international conference on research into higher education, Newport Wales, December 6–8, 2017.

Gaskell, C., & Hayton, E. (2014). *Out in orbit: Strategies and trajectories for higher education satellite campuses.* London: Leadership Foundation for Higher Education. ISBN: 978-1-906627-60-7.

HESA. (2018). Higher Education Statistics Agency. Retrieved from https://www.hesa.ac.uk/data-and-analysis/students/whos-in-he. Accessed on March 1, 2018.

NOMIS. (2011). *NOMIS official labour market statistics.* Office for National Statistics. Retrieved from http://www.nomisweb.co.uk. Accessed on March 1, 2018.

Social Mobility and Child Poverty Commission and Social Mobility Commission. (2016). The Social Mobility Index. Retrieved from https://www.gov.uk/government/publications/social-mobility-index. Accessed on March 1, 2018.

13

A TEACHER'S EXPERIENCE OF THE TRANSFORMATIVE PEDAGOGIC EFFECT OF PART-TIME DEGREE STUDY

Gerard Sharpling and Neil Murray

ABSTRACT

This chapter presents the learning experience of a tutor at a UK university when undertaking a part-time, online degree in Health and Social Care over a seven-year period. Retrospective reflection and sociological theory are applied as methodologies to identify several key challenges faced by mature, widening participation students, involving identity, literacy, workload and assessment. The chapter suggests how an awareness of these issues helps one to empathise more effectively with mature students, the better to promote success and retention. It is suggested that other tutors stand to benefit from engaging in this type of online learning experience to further their own empathy with mature students.

Keywords: Mature students; retention; empathy; online degree; return to study; part-time study

INTRODUCTION

Widening participation (WP) initiatives are an essential part of UK universities' mission and strategy (Field, 2000), serving both as indicators of their ethical credentials and determiners of income. Indeed, in order to charge higher tuition fees, higher education (HE) providers must first have in place an access agreement approved by the Director of Fair Access (OFFA, 2018). However, tutors may have minimal experience of working with students from various WP backgrounds and little understanding of the challenges they may face. By establishing empathy with them, they can make a significant difference to the HE experience of these students (Thomas, Bland, & Duckworth, 2012), enhance their sense of belonging and integration, and increase their own capacity as teachers to accommodate to their students' needs.

This chapter focuses on mature students. It documents some of the experiences gained by one teacher who returned to university to study on a seven year, part-time distance-learning degree programme in Health and Social Care.

METHODOLOGY

The tutor (the first-named author of this paper, hitherto referred to as 'the student') teaches at a UK university and began their on-line degree programme in 2009, when they were also a part-time tutor on a distance learning French programme. As such, the student was reasonably familiar with university procedures but had not previously studied Health and Social Care.

In this ethnographic study, we draw on grounded theory (Strauss & Corbin, 1996) and critical reflection to generate four 'mediating factors' that characterise the student's experience of returning to study: identity, literacy, workload and assessment. These themes emerged as the student reflected more deeply on the entire course of study through a careful reading and re-reading of module websites, emails, student forums and assessment feedback dating back over a seven-year period. The aim of the study is to show how, and what, tutors can learn from this type of educational experience.

CONCEPTUAL MODEL

The structure of learning development that we outline involves (a) the learning experience itself, (b) factors that mediate the learning experience and (c) outcomes in terms of how the experience has transformed our understanding of the learning experiences of certain, though by no means all, WP learners. Whilst studies of how 'role reversal' can enable professional development have been undertaken (see, e.g., Malkiel, 2018; McDonough, 2002), the authors are not aware of any previous studies involving a university tutor undertaking a full part-time degree and evaluating it in this way. Our model is presented in Fig. 1.

We also drew on two sociological theories to inform our understanding of this learning process: Beck's (1992) process of 'disembedding', 'loss of security' and 're-embedding',

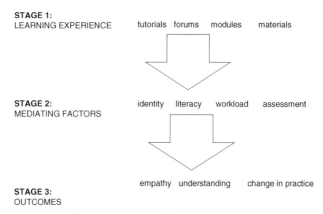

Fig. 1. A Three-stage Model of Tutor Learning through Part-time Study

and Bourdieu's (1984) concept of 'habitus', used to describe the 'norms and practices of social groups' (Thomas, 2002). The relationship between these theories and the themes of identity, workload, literacy and assessment is outlined in the following discussion.

IDENTITY

'Identity' refers to how individuals see themselves as 'belonging', and construct narratives around their experience (Robb, 2007). Crucially, student identity is socially negotiated in a context where identifying a social space for identity can often be challenging (Beattie-Smith, 2017).

The student found that upon returning to study, their established, current, social context came into conflict with a new, competing identity of being a student again in a completely different subject area, leading to a sense of 'disembedding', and potential anxiety. As Thomas and Hanson (2014) argue, the conflict between 'habitus' and the university's behavioural expectations affects students from specific demographic groups, such as mature students, who may find it challenging to access the requisite social and cultural capital to integrate into their new online environment when beginning a programme of study.

Online modules increasingly make use of forums, which enable students and teachers to engage 'virtually' in discussion around their studies, to ask questions, and build a sense of community. The following forum post shows how the student's sense of 'habitus' was initially challenged by having to engage with a module located in an unfamiliar, science-based discipline, which required a completely different approach to studying and writing:

> *Actually, I am struggling a bit with being able to recognise microbes from slides, outside of their very general features, colour and size. Does anyone happen to know if there are any web sites with good pictures of microbes and their associated names?*

This message shows the student's anxiety at being unable to read microbe slides effectively. The sense of being outside one's comfort zone also led to the student questioning their 'legitimacy' in terms of student status: whether they 'should' be following the course; whether they would 'fit in' to the programme and whether they had the skills and ability to successfully complete the module in an unfamiliar, science-based discipline.

Despite initial difficulties in establishing a sense of academic identity within a new area of study, online 'communities of practice' helped to foster greater confidence and self-esteem and dispel anxieties over legitimacy. As Mercieca (2017) has argued, online 'communities of practice' that bring together participants with shared interests can serve as a remedy for isolation. For the student, the availability of this type of online community helped to raise the following study problem in one of their science modules:

> *There was just one calculation that I didn't understand so please could I ask about this? Sorry if it is a silly/obvious question.*

The ability to raise questions did not develop immediately, but depended on a growing sense of confidence around interacting in an online environment. This kind of interaction may not always be possible for students lacking confidence in themselves and in their IT skills, and this can be a cause and consequence of feelings of isolation, thereby affecting student satisfaction (Daugherty & Funke, 1998).

LITERACY

Writing skills are important in any degree programme. However, literacy is a broad concept and what it means to be 'literate' in one field does not automatically guarantee literacy in another (Hyland, 2000; Murray, 2013). The difficulty of developing academic literacy in unfamiliar content areas often arises through the lack of familiarity with the language of the discipline and the requirement to communicate in particular ways' (Butcher et al., 2017). In the case of the student, the key areas of experiential learning here were the need to simplify their writing and make it more direct, and to adapt to and engage in new writing styles and genres associated with a 'foreign' discipline.

Unlike many mature students, the student, working as they were in an academic setting, was likely to be more familiar with the requirements of a piece of academic writing. However, this is not always as advantageous as one might suppose. For example, in early modules, the student's writing – part of their learned behaviour – was sometimes seen by their course tutors as 'difficult' in terms of its level of semantic and lexical complexity. As the modules progressed, the writing process became easier as the student developed a better understanding of the disciplinary requirements and expectations concerning written work, as the following comment suggests:

> *I think I have finally worked out a formula to write effective essays for my Health and Social Care modules. I tend to write using 150 word paragraphs with one paragraph for the introduction and one for the conclusion. I write the bibliography first and then the first sentence of each paragraph, as a paragraph plan (diary entry).*

This extract indicates that as the student gained greater experience through following the modules, they developed an approach to literacy that simplified the writing process and focused more directly on the tasks set.

The student was also required to adapt to different sub-genres of academic writing. Concerns about academic literacy across subject boundaries were encapsulated in the following question, expressed in an email to the student's tutor early in a Science module:

> *Hello. I am a new student on the Science module and am just checking in to say hello. I am not a very experienced scientist (I did O level physics many years ago and have a lot to learn) but I am looking forward to the challenges of the module and have looked ahead a bit at the module materials.*

Despite the anxieties evident here, the following feedback confirmed that the student had in fact coped well with the requisite scientific discourse:

> *This was an excellent assignment, I know you found the chemistry difficult to get to grips with, and you worked really hard on the topic, so the hard work paid off! All questions were well answered, your diagrams were clearly labelled, and you explained things with correct scientific terminology.*

In one third-year module on Youth Studies, however, the feedback received on one essay was less positive, indicating that the student was bringing in too many 'contemporary' examples from outside the module materials and missing out important details from the module books themselves. The student felt unhappy with the feedback and disappointed with their marks, and was thus able to experience first-hand the 'ups and downs' of assignment writing, with its associated successes and disappointments.

WORKLOAD

Mature students are, arguably, more prone to stresses and commitments in their personal lives: these could include childcare or caring for an older relative; long working hours; financial pressures and personal health, all of which can have a disruptive effect on their studies (Kinnear, 2009; Moreau & Leathwood, 2006). A student familiar with the academic environment should be well used to managing tight workloads; however, as the student found, even the best-planned schedule could easily be thrown off course by unforeseen events. The student experienced illness in one of the early modules, leading to their request for a three-week extension to the assignment deadline:

> *Hi everyone, I am sending best wishes from a hospital bed after a severe internal bleed today. Good job I managed to submit my assignment. I am feeling ok, just a little tired and can't do smiley faces with cannula in my left arm (sic).*

It was fortunate that the student's module tutors were supportive and willing to be flexible with essay deadlines and extensions. One tutor, for example, permitted flexibility in the final assessment of one module in order to enable successful completion of the course:

> *I have given you an extension until the 27th April (which is the latest date I can give you). Just submit what you can - like I say you only need a few marks to pass this first half of the course.*

Such interventions are, arguably, positive filters when undertaking an academic course, leading to better outcomes and student retention amongst a cohort that is often more susceptible to the pressures of family commitments, work demands and health issues (Bolam & Dodgson, 2001).

The most time-consuming module for the student was a large (30-point/300-hour Level 1) science module, because its contents were less familiar.[1] The student recalls a forum post they wrote on a rainy bank holiday Monday spent learning how to balance chemical equations and studying the basics of

---

1 The Credit Accumulation and Transfer (CAT) system in the UK is designed to enable students to accumulate credits for study that may be 'transferred' both within and beyond the institution. One credit is equivalent to approximately ten hours of study time.

organic chemistry – skills that do not necessarily come naturally to a modern language specialist:

> *I am enjoying Unit 4 of the book but have had*
> *a few issues with balancing chemical equations.*
> *I've grasped the principles of it and am trying*
> *(very quickly!) to develop the skills of equation*
> *balancing.*

Overall, the student felt that the science module involved much more work than many of the other modules, given their lack of familiarity with the materials.

ASSESSMENT

One particular challenge the student faced whilst studying concerned the submission of several written assignments throughout the year and also final examinations or projects: all to be fitted into a busy work, home and family life with competing demands and loyalties.

They found it instructive to see the assessment process from the point of view of other students. For example, all universities now have strict turnaround times for marking which can create pressure when marking assignments, but seen from the students' perspective, a few days can feel lengthy when awaiting results of examinations or assignments. This point was frequently discussed in forums and on social media pages. For instance, in response to a delay in receiving feedback on one assignment, the student wrote:

> *Well, I think the results are taking their time – I*
> *wonder if they are deciding to add 10 per cent to*
> *all of our scores. Seriously though, I am sure the*
> *results will be ready soon.*

Table 1. Traditional and Developing Views of Key Mediating Factors in the Student's Experience.

Mediating Factor	Traditional View	Evolved View
Identity	Tutor works with a clearly defined 'group' of students.	Student identity is one of many identities that a student possesses; 'belonging' is a constructed, tenuous notion, and can lead to vulnerability.
Literacy	There are fixed ways of producing assignments based on implicit 'rules' about what academic writing should look like.	Academic writing is a 'construct' and neither self-evident nor naturally occurring. A fluid approach to acceptability helps to challenge fixed, sometimes 'elite' notions of knowledge, its construction and articulation.
Workload	Students should have sufficient motivation to carry them through difficult times.	Students face significant challenges in their lives and bureaucratic systems are not always designed to allow for such variability; flexibility is often the key to promote student retention.
Assessment	Students may feel anxious about assessments and examinations because of previous negative learning experiences, but they are an unpleasant fact and a 'rite of passage'.	Students' voices are rarely heard in discussions about testing and assessment; one cannot underestimate the difference that a supportive and flexible assessment system can make in enabling students to produce their best work in assessments.

A further aspect of the student's experience was that the vast majority of assignments were marked positively, and the wording of the feedback was friendly and supportive, and helped to scaffold and develop learning.

No less important was the awareness gained of how assignments were phrased and examination questions constructed. It was noteworthy that attention was given to avoiding ambiguous or unnecessarily complicated language in examination questions. This reinforced the views of the module tutors that examinations were intended to ascertain whether students had read and understood the module materials, and not to catch students out.

OUTCOMES

We conclude this chapter by documenting the actual process of transformative thinking that resulted from the experience of studying on this part-time degree programme and how it has influenced the student's thinking. We set this out as a series of mappings from 'traditional' to 'evolving' approaches to working with students that question commonly held beliefs and attitudes. These mappings have arisen directly through the disruption to – or perhaps, recalibration of – the student's 'habitus', coupled with a process of 'disembodying' and 're-embedding', as articulated by Beck (1992).

The overall transformations are documented in Table 1.

We believe, in conclusion, that based on this research, encouraging tutors to engage in studying an online module as part of their professional development would pay dividends in terms of widening and extending this learning to others.

REFERENCES

Beattie-Smith, G. (2017, April 3). What's App for peer support and community building. A paper presented to the School of Languages and Linguistics (LAL). The Open University. Retrieved from https://learn3.open.ac.uk/mod/oucollaborate/view.php?id=121005. Accessed on September 27, 2017.

Beck, U. (1992). *Risk society: Towards a new modernity*. London: Sage.

Bolam H., & Dodgson, R. (2001). *Widening participation and the role of ICT: Exploring possibilities*. Newcastle: Universities for the North East. Retrieved from http://www.unis4ne.ac.uk/files/Retention_report70.pdf. Accessed on September 27, 2017.

Bourdieu, P. (1984). *Distinction: A social critique of the judgement of taste*. London: Routledge.

Butcher, J., McPherson, E., Shelton, I., Clarke, A., Hills, L., & Hughes, J. (2017). Unfit for purpose? Rethinking the language of assessment for widening participation students. *Widening Participation and Lifelong Learning*, *19*(2), 27–46.

Daugherty, M., & Funke, B. L. (1998). University faculty and student perceptions of Web-based instruction. *Journal of Distance Education*, *13*(1), 21–39.

Field, J. (2000). *Lifelong learning and the new educational order*. Staffordshire: Trentham Books.

Hyland, K. (2000). *Disciplinary discourses: Social interactions in academic writing*. Harlow: Longman.

Kinnear, A. (2009). *Diversity: A longitudinal study of how student diversity relates to resilience and successful progression in a new generation university*. Sydney:

Australian Learning and Teaching Council. Retrieved from http://www.altc.edu.au/system/files/resources/CG6-38_ECU_Kinnear_Final%20ReportApr09.pdf. Accessed on September 29, 2017.

Malkiel, B. (2018). Developing empathy through role reversal: A personal case study. *English Language Teacher Education and Development*, *21*, 10–15.

McDonough, J. (2002). The teacher as language learner: Worlds of difference. *ELT Journal*, *56*(4), 404–411.

Mercieca, B. (2017). What is a community of practice? In J. McDonald & A. Cater-Steel (Eds.), *Communities of practice: Facilitating social learning in higher education*. London: Springer.

Moreau, M., & Heathwood, C. (2006). Balancing paid work and studies: Working-class students in higher education. *Studies in Higher Education*, *31*(1), 23–42.

Murray, N. (2013). Widening participation and English language proficiency: A convergence with implications for assessment practices in higher education. *Studies in Higher Education*, *38*(2), 299–311.

Office for Fair Access. (2018). Introducing access agreements. Retrieved from https://www.offa.org.uk/universities-and-colleges/introducing-access-agreements/. Accessed on February 13, 2018.

Robb, M. (2007). Gender. In M. Kehily (Ed.), *Understanding youth: Perspectives, identities, practices* (pp. 73–106). London: Sage.

Strauss, A., & Corbin, J. (1994). *Grounded theory methodology: Handbook of qualitative research* (pp. 273–285). Thousand Oaks, CA: Sage.

Thomas, B. G., & Hanson, J. (2014). Developing social integration to enhance student retention and success in higher education: The GROW@BU initiative. *Widening Participation and Lifelong Learning*, 16(3), 58–70.

Thomas, L. (2002). Student retention in higher education: The role of institutional habitus. *Journal of Education Policy*, 17(4), 423–442.

Thomas, L., Bland, D., & Duckworth, V. (2012). Teachers as advocates for widening participation. *Widening Participation and Lifelong Learning*, 14(2), 40–55.

SECTION D

ACCESS TO SUCCESS
AND SOCIAL MOBILITY:
THINKING BIG

14

ACCESS TO SUCCESS AND SOCIAL MOBILITY INVOLVES EVERYONE! A WHOLE INSTITUTION APPROACH TO WIDENING PARTICIPATION

Liz Thomas

ABSTRACT

Increasing diversity in higher education (HE) – or widening participation (WP) – is now a concern worldwide (Billingham in this volume, Chapter 1; Bowes, Thomas, Peck, & Nathwani, 2013; Shah, Bennett, & Southgate, 2016). However, we all know that access to HE is not sufficient; access needs to be accompanied by success – staying on the course, gaining a good degree and securing graduate-level employment. In this chapter, it is argued that in order to equalise student outcomes a 'whole institution approach' (WIA) is required. Evidence is drawn from two studies (each led by the author): one focussing on improving student retention and success in HE, which concluded that a WIA is required (Thomas, Hill, O' Mahony, & Yorke, 2017, pp. 133–135). The second commissioned by the Office for Fair Access to better understand a WIA to WP (Thomas, 2017). The chapter discusses three key findings: the importance of both cultural and structural change; the role of evidence and the need for a deliberate process of change. These findings are illustrated with examples.

Keywords: Student success; institutional change; whole institution approach

INTRODUCTION

In England, students from under-represented and non-traditional groups do less well on all outcome indicators than other students (HEFCE, 2013), prompting an on-going concern about differential rates of success. Students from lower socio-economic groups, ethnic minorities[1] and other disadvantaged groups are more likely to withdraw, achieve a less good degree classification and be unemployed or in a non-graduate job. In order to address differential outcomes, the English National Strategy for Access and Student Success (HEFCE and OFFA, 2015) and the Social Mobility Advisory Group (Social Mobility Advisory Group, 2016), both conclude that a whole institution approach (WIA) is required. Experts such as Billingham (2008), Layer (2002) and Thomas (2001) have long been arguing that institutions need to change to meet the needs of new student

---

1 Although rates vary between ethnic minority groups, overall ethnic minorities have less good outcomes than white students.

populations, rather than expecting students to adapt. These prescriptions are informed by research on widening participation (WP) (Moore, Sanders, & Higham, 2013); student retention (Thomas et al., 2017) and student attainment (Mountford-Zimdar et al., 2015) in the UK; and comparable research abroad (e.g. Atherton, Dumangane, & Whitty, 2016; Kift, 2009).

A WIA supports students both across their student journey and in all parts of their HE experience. It can be understood as a transformative institutional approach to WP.[2]

> *The transformative approach looks at changing the HE institution to offer a more relevant and appropriate HE experience. This would include the introduction of new courses and modes of delivery, changes to admissions requirements and processes, student-centred curriculum contents, pedagogy and assessment, and more inclusive organisational structures and cultures to promote and facilitate the engagement of all students. The transformative approach is premised on the principle that diversity is of value to an institution and the students that study there, and thus should be embraced and used to develop positively for the benefit of all students. (Thomas, 2018a)*

Institutional transformation to embed WP and diversity (*or to become an inclusive institution*) is challenging. For example, in 2009 HEFCE requested a strategic assessment from each higher education institution (HEI) of their approach to WP. This showed that limited progress had been made towards a WIA (Thomas et al., 2010).

---

2 As opposed to academic or utilitarian approaches which do not adjust the excluding features of the traditional HE experience (Jones & Thomas, 2005)

STUDY 1: WHAT WORKS? STUDENT RETENTION AND SUCCESS

In 2008, the *What works? Student retention and success programme* (WW?1) was launched. It involved seven projects and 22 HE providers, researching and evaluating interventions to improve student outcomes (Thomas, 2012). Subsequently, a change programme (WW?2) was launched whilst working with 13 universities to implement changes informed by findings from WW?1, and the process and outcomes were evaluated (Thomas et al., 2017).

The first study found that students' engagement and belonging in their academic learning is at the heart of retention and success (Thomas, 2012), subsequently discipline teams were central to the process of developing interventions to improve retention and success in the second programme. Each of the participating institutions identified at least three subject areas in which interventions would be located, and 43 discipline teams participated in the change programme. The evaluation utilised a mixed methodology and operated at different levels and with different purposes (for a fuller methodological description, see Thomas et al., 2017).

STUDY 2: UNDERSTANDING A WIA TO WP

This study was commissioned in 2017 to generate evidence and guidance to assist HEIs to further develop and evaluate their WIA to WP.

The study was designed to answer the following three key questions:

- What is involved in a 'WIA' to WP and fair access?
- How is the thematic work, such as WP, managed across a whole institution?

- What strategies and tools are, or can be, used to evidence impact when thematic work such as WP is implemented across an institution or organisation?

This study was based on five institutional case studies, and a participatory event for the sector to discuss the interpretation of the evidence. It found that at *a minimum*, a WIA involves:

- working across the student lifecycle; providing pre-entry interventions; an inclusive curriculum and on-course support and measures to improve progression beyond graduation;

- engaging staff from across the institution, not just 'professional WP' staff-employed primarily to deliver WP activities or outcomes; and

- a clear and explicit institutional commitment to WP.

This chapter discusses the following three key findings, which are shared across these two studies:

(1) the importance of cultural and structural change;

(2) the role of evidence; and

(3) the need for a deliberate process of change.

CULTURAL AND STRUCTURAL CHANGE

In the WIA study, staff identified many 'soft' characteristics, such as shared attitudes and values, and ways of doing things, that enable students from under-represented and disadvantaged communities to access HE and be successful. There was a belief in the case study institutions that these values, and ways of doing things, were shared across the staff – and in some, the student-body, and this facilitated a WIA.

The WW?2 study (Thomas et al., 2017) found that staff engagement was the most challenging aspect of introducing changes to improve student retention and success. Most interventions were initiated by staff 'champions', who worked hard using a range of formal and informal tactics to engage their colleagues. Relying on committed individuals to improve student participation and success can result in an inconsistent student experience, depending on the part of the institution with which students engage. It can also result in fragmentation, duplication and gaps in provision, and it absolves some staff of responsibility for delivering an institutional priority.

> *Engaging staff remains a significant challenge and reaching a wider group of staff, beyond those immediately involved, remains difficult. None of the strategies tried so far has achieved significant involvement from a wide range of staff. (Project leader interview, Thomas et al., 2017, p. 108)*

Within WW?2, a number of institution-level policies and procedures were identified to promote and facilitate staff engagement: staff work allocation model; staff development and support; opportunities for pedagogical research and development and routes for staff recognition and promotion based on engagement in student success activities.

It was found within the WIA study that a 'top-down, bottom-up approach' (Kift, 2009), which combines structural and cultural elements, is necessary. Culture refers to the values, attitudes and practices of the staff (and students) within the institution; whilst structure refers to the institutional policies, processes and organisation (e.g., of financial and human resources) of the institution and its sub-units. The structure can facilitate the institutional culture (and bottom-up work of staff and students) or frustrate it. Structure can push or 'nudge' people towards the desired culture; it contributes to the consistency of outcomes across the institution. For example, by co-ordinating widening access activities and ensuring an inclusive curriculum across the board.

The interplay of culture and structure – the top-down, bottom-up approach – enables individuals to be sufficiently well-informed and have the capacity and commitment to implement inclusive practices (culture). The structure both helps to ensure this, and provides co-ordination across the institution, promoting integration and consistency – and avoiding duplication, fragmentation and gaps in provision.

Developing and evaluating an institutional structure that promotes WP can be understood to involve:

- ensuring all policies, processes and organisation are designed to take account of WP and diversity;

- considering the extent to which structures are implemented as planned and move beyond paper-based aspirations or statements; and

- assessing the impact of the structure on WP/diverse students.

Developing and evaluating an institutional culture that promotes WP involves:

- raising people's awareness and understanding of the issues;

- developing their skills and capacity to deliver inclusive practice;

- ensuring people develop and deliver inclusive practice; and

- demonstrating the impact of people's practice on the experiences or outcomes of students from target groups.

THE ROLE OF EVIDENCE

In both studies, 'evidence' was found to be vital to the process of institutional transformation. In WW?2, high-quality evidence was used for a range of purposes. Given the complexity of addressing student retention and success, it was found to be necessary to understand local contexts in order to inform the development of suitable interventions. This involved identifying disciplines, courses and modules with lower than expected rates of success (e.g., continuation, progression, completion and attainment); looking at student characteristics or groups with study success issues; and understanding the specific success challenges in each discipline, programme or module in relation to student characteristics. Once this contextual understanding was developed, it could be used to inform the choice of interventions – also informed by institutional or national evidence.

Throughout the implementation, evidence was used to monitor and follow up on individual students' engagement and success to:

- take additional action if required;

- formatively evaluate and develop interventions and approaches and make them more effective; and

- evaluate the impact of interventions on specific groups of students who have lower rates of engagement, belonging, retention or success.

HEIs participating in WW?2 found the project valuable in improving the quality and usability of their institutional data by teaching staff. For example,

> *The Academic Board has noted in its minutes that*
> *the quality of debate around issues of retention,*
> *progression and success has been significantly*

> *improved since the new data reporting structure*
> *was introduced. (Participating institution, Thomas*
> *et al., 2017, p. 96)*

Within the WIA research, case study institutions' data and evidence were used to understand the issues; ensure staff accountability; monitor student experiences and outcomes; inform strategic and operational decision making and evaluate the process and impact of change. Some institutions had developed their monitoring, evaluation and research capacity, either through the integration of data services with WP activities, or more usually through setting-up a specialist unit to investigate issues related to student diversity, and use this knowledge to inform institutional policies and practices.

A DELIBERATE PROCESS OF CHANGE

Developing a WIA to widen participation and diversity is difficult to achieve because HEIs are *complex* systems, with many different individuals and multiple groups contributing in varying ways to the institutional vision of WP – and students' HE experiences and outcomes. Whilst this can be very positive, it can also result in a fragmented and incoherent student experience, with duplication and gaps in provision, and even 'competition' between comparable interventions, resulting in staff frustration and student confusion.

This can be contrasted with a *complicated* system, where there is a fixed – albeit complicated – way in which the institution operates. This provides more certainty in student-facing processes, and the experiences and outcomes for students. This has to be balanced, however, against the value of bottom-up initiatives developed to meet student needs in a local disciplinary context; hence, the earlier recommendation to adopt a 'top-down, bottom-up' approach.

This points to the need for a deliberate process of change, combining cultural and structural changes, aiming towards a *complicated* system, which provides greater consistency across processes, experiences and outcomes for students – underpinned by dissemination and opportunities to share practice. Through WW?2, different approaches to implementing change were uncovered, but they suggest a number of shared features.

A structured approach to organise and manage change is useful, but sufficient time is required. In particular, it is valuable to assess institutional readiness for change, taking into consideration the extent to which leadership at all levels is on board. Institutional structures must be aligned with the desired changes, and good quality data are available in a user-friendly format.

A cross-institutional team, with clear roles and operating at different levels within the institution, is vital. The team needs to play a range of roles, such as:

- coordinating and supporting the work of others across the institution;

- providing data and supporting evaluation;

- engaging with the wider institution to raise awareness and understanding; and ultimately

- changing wider practices.

Involving students in the process of change is highly beneficial.

Ensuring staff engagement is essential but challenging. Leadership is required at all levels (Thomas, 2018b), and explicit senior management support is crucial (see Willcocks in this volume, Foreword). Reporting on the change process and associated outcomes raises awareness of the importance of WP and informs debate, policy and practice within the institution, and provides opportunities for others to learn and develop:

> *Through the committee structure, the institution*
> *was able to review progress on the individual*
> *projects, but more importantly to gain the benefit*
> *of exposure to the principles behind 'What Works?'*
> *This in turn has helped to inform the strategies*
> *being adopted across the institution for the next*
> *academic year to support retention. (Participating*
> *institution, Thomas et al., 2017, p. 104)*

EXAMPLES

Here are three composite examples of ways in which institutions are working to deliver a WIA to WP across the student lifecycle, and illustrating the themes identified in this chapter.

Collaborative and Co-ordinated Outreach Involving Staff and Students from across the Institution

Academic staff, careers advisers and students contribute to outreach work in schools to:

- raise awareness of HE;

- inform decision making;

- develop understanding of new subjects;

- improve academic expectations;

- create links with existing students; and

- offer support and provide careers' planning.

Staff time and funding is allocated to different departments in the institution to facilitate this. Sharing experiences across the institution means people learn from each other; staff and students initiate activities because they are committed to and have the expertise to undertake outreach work. Support and direction are offered by the strategic lead for diversity. The activities are co-ordinated by a central office to avoid schools being contacted multiple times by the HEI.

Addressing Differential Attainment

Institutional research demonstrates that students from ethnic minority groups have lower attainment compared to comparable white students; thus, institutional leaders make reducing the attainment-differential a priority. A key performance indicator is introduced and all staff undergo training and capacity development regarding inclusive learning, teaching and assessment. This includes the introduction of sessions to unpack and improve understanding of each assignment brief. Staff use these tools to change their learning, teaching and assessment practices; in addition, they are monitored, as are the student outcomes.

Improving Employment Outcomes

Institutional research demonstrates that work placements improve employment outcomes for non-traditional students. The institution makes explicit to staff, students and families its commitment to placements. Discussion of placements is integrated into outreach and recruitment activities, and throughout the first two years of study. Students who have been on placement are trained as peer mentors who subsequently support other students to go on a placement; and additional financial support is available for low-income students. Work placements are built into all courses, and academic staff are engaged in the process.

CONCLUSIONS

In the English context, policy and practice is moving from projects designed to widen access to a WIA intended to both widen participation and equalise student experiences and outcomes. Whilst previous research has demonstrated that a WIA better serves students from under-represented and non-traditional groups, it is challenging to achieve.

Evidence from the two studies has been used to illustrate the following three themes:

- the dual need for cultural and structural change (a 'top-down, bottom-up' approach);

- the role of evidence throughout the process; and

- the value of a deliberate process of change aiming to deliver an effective student experience and outcomes for all students.

Institutions that are serious about widening access – and supporting student success – should plan to introduce a deliberate process of change, designed to bring about both cultural and structural change, underpinned by data, research and evaluation. The aim needs to be to move beyond empowering individuals to take action towards the common goal of WP, to the development of a *complicated* organisational system which is informed by on-going innovation, development and evaluation. This is rolled out more broadly to support a 'consistent-as-possible' student experience and ensure equality of outcomes for all students, irrespective of demographic characteristics or subject studied.

There is a difficult balance to be achieved between staff ownership and innovation on the one-hand, and development and improvement across the entirety of the institution for all students, on the other. The first steps, however, are to understand what is required to plan a deliberate process of institutional change and put in place the data and evidence to inform and support the process.

REFERENCES

Atherton, G., Dumangane, C., & Whitty, G. (2016). *Charting equity in higher education: Drawing the global access map*. London: Pearson.

Billingham, S. (2008). Old dogs and new tricks: Skills, lifelong learning and higher education. *Forum for Access and Continuing Education – The Organisation for Lifelong Learning*, No. 30, Summer.

Bowes, L., Thomas, L., Peck, L., & Nathwani, T. (2013). *International research on the effectiveness of widening participation report to HEFCE and OFFA*. Bristol: HEFCE.

HEFCE. (2013). *Higher education and beyond. Outcomes from full-time first degree study*. 2013/15. Bristol: HEFCE.

HEFCE, & OFFA. (2015). *National strategy for access and student success*. London: Department for Business, Innovation and Skills. Retrieved from http://www.hefce. ac.uk/sas/nsass/

Jones, R., & Thomas, L. (2005). The 2003 UK Government higher education white paper: A critical assessment of its implications for the access and widening participation agenda. *Journal of Education Policy*, *20*(5), 615–630.

Kift, S. M. (2009). *Articulating a transition pedagogy to scaffold and to enhance the first year student learning experience in Australian higher education*. Final Report for ALTC Senior Fellowship Program. ALTC Resources.

Retrieved from http://www.altc.edu.au/resource-first-year-learning-experience-kift-2009. Accessed on February 7, 2010.

Layer, G. (2002). Developing inclusivity. *International Journal of Lifelong Learning*, 21(1), 3–12.

Moore, J., Sanders, J., & Higham, L. (2013). *Literature review of research into widening participation to higher education*. Bristol: HEFCE.

Mountford-Zimdars, A., Sabri, D., Moore, J., Sanders, J., Jones, S., & Higham, L. (2015). *Causes of differences in student outcomes*. Bristol: HEFCE.

Shah, M., Bennett, A., & Southgate, E. (Eds.). *Widening higher education participation. A global perspective*. Kidlington: Elsevier.

Social Mobility Advisory Group. (2016). *Working in partnership: Enabling social mobility in higher education. The final report of the social mobility advisory group*. London: Universities UK.

Thomas, L. (2001). *Widening participation in post-compulsory education*. London: Continuum Books.

Thomas, L. (2012). *Building student engagement and belonging in higher education at a time of change: Final report from the what works? Student retention & success programme*. London: Paul Hamlyn Foundation.

Thomas, L. (2017). *Understanding a whole institution approach to widening participation*. Bristol: Office for Fair Access.

Thomas, L. (2018a forthcoming). Governing access and recruitment in higher education: An institutional perspective. In *Encyclopedia of International Higher Education Systems and Institutions*. London: Springer International.

Thomas, L. (2018b forthcoming). Leadership for institutional change to promote diversity and success. in

Thomas, L., Hill, M., O' Mahony, J., & Yorke, M. (2017). *Supporting student success: Strategies for institutional change. What works? Student retention and success programme. Final report.* London: Paul Hamlyn Foundation.

Thomas, L., Storan, J., Wylie, V., Berzins, K., Harley, P., Linley, R., & Rawson, A. (2010). *Review of widening participation strategic assessments.* Ormskirk: Action on Access. Retrieved from https://www.heacademy.ac.uk/system/files/review_of_wp_assessments-2009.pdf

15

ADVOCATING FOR ACCESS: WORLD ACCESS TO HIGHER EDUCATION DAY AND BEYOND

Graeme Atherton

ABSTRACT

Higher education (HE) should be at the forefront of attempts to navigate a route through the confluence of disruptive forces affecting the world in the early twenty-fist century. The early part of the century has seen inequality, in particular, return to the fore. In its survey of over 200 global experts worldwide, the World Economic Forum (2017) stated that:

> *Growing income and wealth disparity is seen by respondents as the trend most likely to determine global developments over the next 10 years. (p. 11)*

Yet, HE remains a bastion of inequality increasingly obsessed with rankings, which openly celebrate elitism in an era where elites are increasingly derided. Fostering inequality and celebrating elitism are becoming high-risk strategies in the midst of the post-crash populism of the 2010s. There are other routes open to what HE can be; safer and better ones for HE itself. However, it will take global advocacy and action if they are to be followed. This chapter presents the key evidence for, and a model, for such advocacy.

Keywords: Global evidence; global advocacy; access to success

INTRODUCTION

There is a growing global knowledge base where inequalities in higher education (HE) participation is concerned. Atherton, Dumangane, and Whitty (2016) examined the quality and extent of the data available on who participates in HE across the world. It showed that in all countries in the world where data are available (which is over 90%), there is an evidence of differences in participation by social background. Comparing countries is difficult. There are comparative data sets available (e.g., from the OECD, World Bank and the European Commission); however, they only cover certain countries. They also focus primarily on proxy measures of socio-economic background such as parental occupation or income. Except for gender and socio-economic background, the majority of countries do not collect any more data on different dimensions of inequality. Moreover, for many countries – in the global south especially – data on participation by socio-economic background are sparse.

However, the universal presence of HE access inequalities remains. Recent research on 31 European countries undertaken via the EU Statistics on Income and Living Conditions

(EU-SILC) project shows that, on average, young adults (25–34 years old) with at least one parent who has completed tertiary education are nearly three times as likely to complete tertiary education themselves as those who have parents with upper secondary or post-secondary non-tertiary education as their highest level of education.

From countries in the global south, there is also evidence of inequality in access by socio-economic background. Analysis of the World Bank data from nine countries in south-east Asia found that, on average, children whose parents have participated in tertiary education are 20% more likely to go on to such education themselves than those whose parents had only an upper-secondary education.[1] Looking at Africa, exclusively in Ghana, those in the richest fifth of the population are seven times more likely to go to HE than those in the poorest two fifths (Atuahene & Owsu-Ansah, 2013).

For those countries driving the global increase in HE students, that is, China and India, the data show how socio-economic background interacts with other forms of inequality, such as geography. In China – the country with one in five of all students in the world – those from poor, rural backgrounds are seven times less likely to enter HE compared to poor students living in urban areas (China Daily, 2016; Hongbin, Loyalka, Rozelle, Wu, & Xie, 2013).

In India, where there are over 300 million students, the picture is even more striking: those in the highest income groups are over 20 times more likely to enter HE than those in the poorest. The gap becomes even wider when gender and geography are considered, with poor, rural females 40 times less likely to go to HE compared to wealthy, urban males

---

1 Available at http://siteresources.worldbank.org/EDUCATION/Resources/ 278200-1221666119663/5381544-1273600002227/equity_in_tertiary_ education.htm.

(Tilak, 2015). This is in part because those for whom access should be widened is defined differently across the world. As Clancy and Goastellec (2007) argue, how access is defined is grounded in the social and political context of that nation.

There are then, perhaps, some potential grounds for optimism where the collection of data is concerned. However, the improvements in such data collection depend critically on political action.

THE NEED FOR POLITICAL COMMITMENT

There is evidence at the level of aspiration, at least, of a commitment to addressing inequalities in access to HE. It is, as pointed out in the Introduction to this volume, one of UNESCO's Global Goals.

In 2015, over 30 European countries committed themselves to setting measurable targets for widening overall participation by 2015 (European Commission/EACEA/Eurydice, 2015). In Latin America, the issue of equity in HE participation features prominently in the debate about the purpose of HE, and across the continent national governments are focussing efforts on widening access. As Ferreyra, Avitabile, Álvarez, Haimovich, and Francisco (2017) state:

> *there has been remarkable progress in the region in terms of expanding higher education access to disadvantaged groups. While the poorest 50 percent of the population (B50) represented only around 16 percent of higher education students circa 2000, this group comprised approximately 25 percent of higher education students circa 2012. By 2012, an additional 3 million B50 young people had gained access to higher education compared with 2000. (p. 79)*

Looking at individual countries, there is evidence from across continents of policy commitments in this area (Atherton et al., 2016). The work of the major English-speaking nations of the UK, the United States and the Australia is well documented. However, the two countries in the world with the largest student populations are also actively involved in widening access work. China is supporting work to increase the number of students entering HE from rural backgrounds by over 100,000 (People's Daily, 2017); and, in India, there is a quota system in place, which allocates places to students from lower castes (Tilak, 2015). The picture painted previously is encouraging but a little digging below the surface reveals a more fragile situation.

In Europe, despite 34 European countries committing to setting measurable targets for widening overall participation by 2015, as stated earlier, only six had done so. It is obviously welcome to see access central to the SDGs, but the way in which access for all is being measured is in terms of gender only. The commitments of individual countries have also been criticised for lacking rigour or being inadequate in the face of some of the challenges facing under-represented/marginalised groups; for example, related to the cost of HE or in the context of broader structural inequalities in the system. The best example of the former case is the United States with its Trillion-Dollar student debt mountain (Friedman, 2014). For the latter, South Africa exemplifies a system constructed on inequality and where access efforts have to be part of a wider transformation agenda (Heleta, 2016).

WORLD ACCESS TO HIGHER EDUCATION DAY (WAHED)

Accepting the fragility of commitments to widening access, there is enough activity to merit attempts at coherent advocacy.

An effective case for change needs to be based on a critical mass of interest in a cause or issue to tap into. That appears to exist. However, there is no agency or organisation, which is linking these efforts together or building a dialogue in the global public space. Strong advocacy, which has access as its defining raison d'etre only, really exists in the United States with the work, for example, of the Council for Opportunity in Education.[2] The long-standing European Access Network has done sterling work bringing practitioners together over recent decades, but little on advocacy.

The rationale for a WAHED, based around similar global commemoration days, is both practical and conceptual. Advocacy efforts are frequently based around a single location event to focus global attention. This approach is difficult in the access space as the activists in the community are dispersed and mostly unable to tap into financial support for travel. Conceptually, a WAHED creates a more open space within which a plurality of voices can be heard.

The aim of WAHED is to create a platform, which raises global awareness around inequalities in HE, and acts as catalyst for local action. It will be based around simultaneous 'hub events' in each continent of the world; with activities designed to break down the barriers to access; and with as many countries as possible taking place on the day. In the build-up to WAHED, the voices of students will be key as those from low income and marginalised communities tell their stories about HE and the impact it has had on their lives. Most importantly, however, the goal is for WAHED to be a springboard for an ongoing global campaign that can promote equitable access to HE.

---

2   For more on the work of the COE, please access: http://www.coenet.org/

HOW CAN WAHED BE EFFECTIVE?

The case for WAHED, and what it represents, may be robust; however, in order to have an impact, it needs to absorb the learning from other efforts at global advocacy inside and outside HE. This requires a number of factors from the outset.

• *Global representation*

The widening access to HE agenda is primarily an Anglo-Western construct. Whilst inequalities prevail everywhere and much work is going on to address these across the world, the language of access and the significant policy investments are found only in certain nations. This puts the responsibility on them to provide the stimulus for global networking – but they cannot dominate. Hence, the governing structure of any initiative such as WAHED must involve representatives from all continents.

• *Access needs to mean success in and through HE*

The importance of students from access backgrounds achieving their potential in HE, and progressing to positive post-HE outcomes, is unquestionable. There is a strong element of expediency in using the label 'access' in an endeavour such as this. However, whilst the expediency case is self-evident, language matters, and so does ensuring that access is interpreted in the terms expressed in the heading to this bullet point, and the title of this book.

• *A platform with goals*

WAHED, and whatever comes from it, has to aspire to a tangible goal that affects the lives of students. Providing the space to exchange practice or do some of the intellectual work required to position access in the academic and policy discourse is important, but WAHED needs to do more than this if it is to gain a global foothold.

- *Engagement of HEIs*

International HE networks have expressed interest in widening access before, as have the supra-national bodies such as the OECD and European Commission noted earlier. The engagement of such bodies is important as well as efficient, but HEIs themselves have to be involved. Regional and national HE networks, whilst having influence, depend on institutions themselves who command many times more resources and power. Many HEIs aspire to global leadership and excellence but few, if any, have yet to articulate this in terms of access. If WAHED and associated efforts are to make an impact, we need some HEIs to do this.

- *Advocacy before academia*

Many academic staff are also passionate and effective advocates who use their expert knowledge to engender change. But, it has also been argued that the reflexive nature of academic training does not pre-dispose them, necessarily, to advocacy. Engaging those involved in learning, teaching and research must be integral to WAHED and subsequent efforts. If such work is seen as the remit only of non-academics, it will struggle to really permeate HE. Any cultural hesitancy regarding advocacy needs to be overcome. Hence, in looking for models from which to take ideas and inspiration, WAHED must look outside academia to campaigning efforts in the wider inequalities/social justice space.

SO, WHERE TO FROM HERE?

Where does such a campaign start? Ambitious goals are needed. A pledge from governments and HE providers to reduce gaps in participation by those from lower socio-economic backgrounds by 30%, by 2035, would be a start. Many HE providers would argue that they do not have data on who enters HE by socio-economic background. For some, there is nothing preventing them collecting such data aside from the will to do so. For others, there may be larger cultural or political barriers.

In those cases, they can identify locally defined inequality where data are readily available (such as 'race' in South Africa or rurality in Kenya). For governments, there is an increasing amount of data available particularly using proxy measures of socio-economic background. The biggest barrier here is political will, which is exactly why WAHED is so crucial. The propensity for 'backsliding' seen in Europe, as described previously, highlights the need for a global campaign that can work with existing international education organisations such as the EC, ASEAN, OECD, etc., to monitor progress against the pledge and keep it in the public eye.

The 30% pledge is the start but there is also huge scope for an active global conversation on how, as HE expands, it does so equitably; enabling HEIs and countries from across the world to learn from each other. HE is a relatively well-connected sector, which benefits from a myriad of trans-national networks at regional and global level. *Yet such knowledge creation is not happening where equity and access is concerned.*

Finally, it also has to include other stakeholders and, in particular, employers. Graduate unemployment is so high in certain countries as to weaken, perhaps even eliminate, the case for equitable access (Bothwell, 2016). As argued earlier, the term access cannot refer just to entry, but must include learners achieving their potential when in HE by successfully completing their courses and progressing to positive post-HE destinations. Employers must be part of this campaign, and leading ones pressed to publish data about the social composition of their workforces.

Addressing inequality in the education system and leaving it untouched in the labour market will only lead to frustrations, which could easily find their outlet in unsettling and negative ways. Part of the catalyst for recent unrest in the Middle East, for example, was relatively well-educated young people frustrated at their lack of economic opportunities.

The need for WAHED and a global campaign on equitable access is compelling. For a long time in the twentieth century, it was thought that there should be limits on how many young people participated in primary or secondary education.[3] Looking back over the past century, these ideas seem a distant memory, but they acted to entrench inequality. Limiting higher education in the same way will further entrench inequality into the twenty-second century.

REFERENCES

Atherton, G. (Ed.). (2016). *Access to higher education: Understanding global inequalities*. London: Palgrave MacMillan.

Atherton, G., Dumangane, C., & Whitty, G. (2016). *Charting equity in higher education: Drawing the global access map*. London: Pearson.

Atuahene, F., & Owusu-Ansah, A. (2013). A descriptive assessment of higher education access, participation, equity, and disparity in Ghana. *SAGE Open, July-September 2013, 1–16*.

---

3   In the UK, raising of the school leaving age was opposed in both 1947 and 1972 (http://www.nationalarchives.gov.uk/cabinetpapers/themes/new-legislation-1944.htm). For an account of the debate here, see Oreopoulos (2005). https://www.cdhowe.org/sites/default/files/attachments/research_papers/mixed/commentary_223.pdf.

Bothwell, E. (2016). Asian HE expansion 'producing more graduates than market needs'. *Times Higher Education.* February 2. Retrieved from http://www. timeshighereducation.com/news/asian-he-expansion-producing-more-graduates-market-needs.

China Daily. (2016). *China has 1 in 5 of all college students in the world.* Report, April 8, 2016.

Clancy, P., & Goastellec, G. (2007). Exploring access and equity in higher education: Policy and performance in a comparative perspective. *Higher Education Quarterly, 61*(2), 136–154.

European Commission/EACEA/Eurydice. (2015). *The European higher education area in 2015: Bologna process implementation report.* Luxembourg: Publications Office of the European Union.

Ferreyra, M., Avitabile, C., Álvarez, J. B., Haimovich P., & Francisco, U. S. (2017). *At a crossroads: Higher education in Latin America and the Caribbean. Directions in development; human development.* Washington, DC: World Bank Group.

Friedman, D. (2014). Americans owe $1.2 trillion in student loans, surpassing credit card and auto loan debt totals. *New York Daily News*, May 17, 2014. Retrieved from http://www.nydailynews.com/news/national/american s-owe-1-2-trillion-student-loans-article-1.1796606

Heleta, S. (2016). Decolonisation of higher education: Dismantling epistemic violence and Eurocentrism in South Africa. *Transformation in Higher Education, 1*, 1.

Hongbin, K., Loyalka, P., Rozelle, S., Wu, B., & Xie, J. (2013, April 26). Unequal access to college in China: How far have poor, rural students been left behind? Working Paper. Rural Education Action Project.

Oreopoulos, P. (2005). *Stay in school: New lessons on the benefits of raising the legal school leaving age.* Toronto, Canada: CD Howe Institute.

People's Daily. (2017, September 1). More China's rural youngsters entering the nation's best universitie. Retrieved from http://en.people.cn/n3/2017/0901/c90000-9263447.html

Tilak, J. (2015). How inclusive is higher education in India? *Social Change, 45*(2), 185–223.

World Economic Forum. (2017). *The global risks report 2017* (12th ed.). Geneva: World Economic Forum.

INDEX

Note: Page numbers followed by "*n*" with numbers indicates footnotes.